CHURCH REFORMS

IN RUSSIA

1905 - 1918

In Commemoration of the 50th Anniversary of the
All-Russian Church Council of 1917-1918

ALEXANDER A. BOGOLEPOV

PUBLICATIONS COMMITTEE OF THE METROPOLITAN COUNCIL OF THE
RUSSIAN ORTHODOX CHURCH OF AMERICA

1520 East Main Street, Bridgeport, Connecticut, U.S.A.

Printed by
Keystone Publishing Co., Berwick, Pennsylvania

contents

Church Reforms In Russia 1905 - 1918*

A. A. BOGOLEPOV

I

Projects of the Eighteenth and Nineteenth Centuries

On JANUARY 25, 1721, the Emperor Peter I issued a manifesto which radically altered the organization of the Russian Church. The authority of the Patriarch was abolished and in his place there was established an Ecclesiastical College made up of persons appointed by the Emperor. For several years prior to 1721, and under the direction of the Emperor himself, Bishop Feofan Prokopovich had been compiling a new body of governing regulations for the Church, called "The Ecclesiastical Reglement." The Reglement was rather hastily examined and then approved by the supreme governing body in the State at that time, the Ruling Senate, in its meetings of January 23rd and 24th, 1721, which were attended also by a number of bishops and archmandrites. Soon after this, in fact on February 14th of the same year, the Ecclesiastical College was re-named The Most Holy Ruling Synod. This name reflected the desire to place the new body on the same level in ecclesiastical affairs as that of the Ruling Senate in civil matters.

In the beginning the Holy Synod was made up of three bishops, four archmandrites and four archpriests. All matters were to be determined by a majority vote, even though the bishops were very much in the minority. No matter what the decisions of the Synod might be, however, they were subject to the control of the state power. Unlike the Patriarch, the members of the Synod were not permitted any direct access to the Emperor. An Ober-Procurator, appointed by the Emperor, was placed as an intermediary between the Emperor and the Holy Synod. As the "eye of the Emperor" the Ober-Procurator participated in all meetings of the Synod, made certain

---

* Translated from the Russian by A. E. Moorhouse.

that its affairs were conducted in accordance with the Ecclesiastical Reglement, and could protest decisions of the Synod which were not in harmony
with the laws and interests of the State, block their implementation, and
bring such matters, together with his own conclusions, to the attention of the
Emperor. Not only did the ratification of the Synod's decrees come to depend
in fact on the Ober-Procurator, but also appointments of new members to
the Synod itself.

This reduction of ecclesiastical authority and its subordination to secular
power came as a painful blow to the clergy of the Russian Church. Indeed
it was not easy for Peter the Great to win acceptance of the reforms which
he introduced. Having persuaded the senators, six bishops and three archmandrites to subscribe to the Ecclesiastical Reglement, and after signing it
himself, he had to resort to formal imperial commands and threats in order
to get the signatures of the more than seventy other church officials—bishops,
archmandrites, abbots and archpriests. The Emperor had no difficulty, however, in obtaining approval from the Eastern Patriarchs of this degradation
of the Russian Church. In 1723 the Patriarchs of Constantinople and Antioch declared the Synod to be their "brother in Christ," "having the right
to execute and establish those things which are done also by the four Most
Holy Patriarchal Apostolic Sees." This acceptance of the Synod by the
Eastern Patriarchs strengthened its position as the collective head of the
Russian Church in its dealings with other Orthodox Local Churches, but
it did nothing to relieve the painful sense of injury within Russia.

It was not long before the author of the Ecclesiastical Reglement himself, Metropolitan Feofan Prokopovich, submitted a proposal for the reorganization of the Synod to Empress Anna Ivanovna (1730-1740). It was
his desire that the number of bishops in the Synod be increased and that
some of its members be "permanent," i.e., independent of the Ober-
Procurator with regard to their removal. This project was not realized. No
sooner had Empress Elizaveta Petrovna (1741-1761) risen to the throne
than two members of the Synod, Archbishop Ambrosy Yushkevich and
Metropolitan Arseny Matsyevich, addressed another memorandum to the
Sovereign concerning the abolition of the synodal form of ecclesiastical
administration, with its office of Ober-Procurator as a secular official within
the Synod. Their memorandum referred also to the Patriarchate as the
ideal form of ecclesiastical administration. Once again the proposal had no
practical consequences.[1]

The system of State administration of ecclesiastical affairs was consolidated more and more, although the Russian Emperors did not interfere in
dogmatic questions as did the Byzantine Basileis. The power of the Ober-

6

Procurator constantly increased, until he became in fact a Minister of State. This process ended in the creation, under Emperor Alexander I, of a Ministry of Ecclesiastical Affairs and Education, which rather alarmed the hierarchy. Metropolitan Mikhail of Novgorod wrote to the Emperor saying that the Church was being threatened and subjected to persecution. By the time the letter actually reached the Emperor in Leibach, the aged Metropolitan had already died. Archmandrite Photius was another opponent of this "twofold Ministry," which in fact existed only for a short time—from 1817 to 1824. Archmandrite Photius hailed its abolition with the words: "Our only Minister is Jesus Christ our Lord."[2]

At the end of the reign of Alexander I there is a noticeable shift from a general criticism of the synodal structure to concrete proposals for the gradual restoration of the authority of the hierarchy. The name of Metropolitan Filaret of Moscow is associated with this new trend. Emperor Alexander I proposed organizing all the Russian provinces *(gubernia)* into nine larger administrative districts *(general-gubernatorstvo)*, each headed by a Governor-General, to whom the Governors within each district would be subordinated. At the same time he gave Metropolitan Filaret the task of drawing up a plan for the harmonization of ecclesiastical and civil administration. In Filaret's plan all the dioceses were also to be organized into nine metropolitan districts *(okrugi)*, in which the authority of the diocesan bishops would be subordinated to that of a Metropolitan. Following the example of Metropolitan districts in the ancient Church, the bishops would assemble at district councils *(sobors)* under the presidency of the Metropolitan for the handling of all local matters. In this way self-governing Metropolitan districts would be created outside governmental control, somewhat limiting the sphere in which the central authority of the Holy Synod could operate. As far as we can judge from the testimony of persons close to Metropolitan Filaret, he believed that the formation of these Metropolitan districts could lead in the future to the creation of an institution having authority even over the Synod. An assembly of twenty-four senior bishops, coming from places at a considerable distance from St. Petersburg, could be regarded as such an institution, which would have power to review complaints regarding the judicial (but not administrative) decisions of the Holy Synod, in cases where the Synod had acted as a judge of the first instance (for example, in the case of a complaint filed against a bishop).[3] This would have marked the beginning of a local *(pomestny)* Council (Sobor) of Bishops of the Russian Church.

Having received Filaret's proposal for the formation of Metropolitan districts, Emperor Alexander, just before his departure for Taganrog, forwarded it with a number of other papers to Arakcheev. After the death of Alexander I Filaret's plan was brought to the knowledge of the members of the Synod, but of course under Emperor Nicolas I it was impossible even to raise the question of a decentralization of ecclesiastical administration.

Metropolitan Filaret's proposal came to the fore again at the time of the passage of the liberal reforms of Emperor Alexander II. The question of the Synod was a subject of lively debate in a private correspondence between a group of highly placed persons. This correspondence was begun by A. N. Muravyev, who served for a time in the Synod as one of the closest aides to the Ober-Procurator. He prepared a memorandum criticizing the synodal system, in which he made a point of saying that the Ober-Procurator had been transformed from a "guardian of the law" into a person having powers in ecclesiastical matters unheard of even for a Patriarch. Muravyev connected the unchecked power of the Ober-Procurator, however, with the "silence of the bishops" and with the intimidation, insufficient education and poverty of the clergy, which had become, in his words, a kind of "dead caste." As a way out of this situation he suggested the limiting of the power of the Ober-Procurator to the preservation of the law and the establishment of mutual relationships between the bishops of the Church, at councils involving groups of dioceses, and also at a Local Council (Sobor) of the Church.

Metropolitan Filaret considered Muravyev's "indictments" of the clergy "exaggerated" but at the same time conceded the need for improving their wretched material conditions. The Metropolitan has himself at one time been dismissed from the Synod by the Ober-Procurator, and so from his own bitter experience did not anticipate anything good coming from a preservation of the authority of the Ober-Procurator as the contact between Church and State. He welcomed the idea of a "mutual concord" between ecclesiastical and State authority, as a willing cooperation of equal partners. As a sound politician, Metropolitan Filaret wanted above all to achieve the real unity of the Episcopate, and to do this without the participation of government authority, thus laying the foundation for independent ecclesiastical administration, which in the future might even lead to a true Bishops' Council. In urging the idea of a council in his correspondence with Muravyev, Filaret again returns to his earlier "plan" for the formation first of all of Metropolitan districts and the setting up of permanent channels of communication between the bishops of dioceses and their district Metropolitan. In cooperation with the latter, according to Filaret, they could manage the affairs of diocesan administration in such a way as not "to be subjected to the undue influence of the proficient members of the consistory and its secretary." The projected calling of a Local Council he put off to a later time. This proposal could be fruitful, he felt, "if handled skillfully and properly."[4] Filaret placed his plan for self-governing Metropolitan Districts at the center of his projected reforms as a parallel to the introduction of local *(zemstvo)* self-government. Only after this plan had been carried out, in his opinion, would it be possible to think about the completion of the reform in the creation of a general council of all bishops.

II

The Revival of the Idea of Conciliarity (Sobornost) in the Nineteenth Century

THE MAKE-UP OF THE Holy Synod was changed several times. A law dated July 8th, 1819, ruled finally that it be composed of seven members. The ratio of bishops to archmandrites and archpriests was also modified, with the number of bishops being gradually increased. In the second half of the 19th century archimandrites and archpriests were no longer invited to participate in the meetings of the Synod, and it became an exclusively episcopal body. The proposals of Metropolitan Filaret clearly indicate the growing significance of the episcopate and his desire to protect episcopal authority in the Church from the oppressive influence of secular power. During the sixties criticism of the synodical system and support for the idea of a Council began to be expressed among the higher clergy with increasing force and insistence. From a letter of Metropolitan Arseny of Kiev to Archbishop Platon of Kostroma, and from the correspondence of Bishop Innokenty (later Metropolitan of Moscow) with A. N. Muravyev, it is clear how deeply disturbed the bishops were by their "subjection to secular power," and how much they were tormented by the knowledge that "the very best proposals, essential to the welfare of the Church, were not being received (by the authorities)."[5] A far more blunt criticism of the developed synodal system was advanced by Archbishop Agafangel of Vyatka (later of Volhynia) in the first years of the reign of Alexander II. The idea of the supremacy of the episcopate and of its independence from secular power in the administration of the Church is the main theme of his memorandum *O plenenii Tserkvi* "The captivity of the Church," which was submitted to the Emperor himself.[6] Archbishop Agafangel wrote: "As the lawful guardians of the treasures deposited by God in the Church, the bishops are crushed by the yoke of an alien power in the execution of their work; although they are silent, they cannot fail to recognize the unlawfulness of this power." He states that even under Peter I, who founded the Synod as a council of bishops and archmandrites, "power over the Church ascended, as it has always done, through the bishops to the Son of God Himself, the one Head of the Church." But the actions of the Ober-Procurator "suppress the hierarchy," "destroy the spirit of the Church" and "turn it into a dying body, gradually giving up its breath and vital functions." At the time of the liberation of the peasants from their bondage to the landlords Archbishop Agafangel made this urgent plea: "Your Majesty! Protasov (the Ober-Procurator) has become the landlord of the bishops, and all the bishops have long become the serfs of the Ober-Procurator and his attendants . . . Show justice to the Holy Church! That justice which you do not withhold from the least of your subjects . . . Have mercy on your subjects! By means of your parental authority, do away with the grievious consequences of this manifest evil!" The conclusions which Archbishop Agafangel drew from this formative position appeared in another memorandum, entitled *Vysshaya administratsia Russkoy Tserkvi* ("The Supreme Administration of the Russian Church"). His view was that the Holy Synod should be transformed into a permanent Holy Ruling All-Russian Church Council.[7]

In the middle of the nineteenth century questions of ecclesiastical life began to be discussed with interest also in various secular circles. In connection with a general development of religious education, articles began to appear in ecclesiastical and also secular journals on administrative and judicial reforms in the department of Orthodox Church Affairs. These reforms were to be carried out "according to the principles of Ecumenical Conciliar legislation," i.e., in the light of the canons of the ancient Church. One outstanding article on the central organs of the Church was *O sobornom upravlenii v Khristianskoy Tserkvi* ("Conciliar Administration in the Christian Church"), published in *Chteniya v imperatorskom obshchestve istorii i drevnostey Rossiiskikh* ("Papers of the Imperial Society of Russian History and Antiquity"), Vol. 4, 1870. According to the plan set forth in this article, there should be formed at the lowest level of conciliarity, i.e., in each diocese, "conferences of persons elected by the clergy and laity," which would decide certain matters subject to the ratification of the diocesan bishop, while submitting other matters to the decision of a District Council of Bishops (or Council of the Metropolia). Out of this intermediate "level," matters would be transferred to a greater Council, i.e., to the Holy Synod, where together with appointed members there should be present also bishops chosen by the District Councils. This article reflects the familiar and still influential idea of Metropolitan Filaret concerning the restoration of the ancient Metropolitan districts (see First Ecumenical Council, Canons IV, VI). At the same time it provides a definite structure for the supreme hierarchical body. In these plans, however, practical considerations obviously prevail over strict adherence to the canons. The rule that Metropolitan districts be closely related to the administrative system of the Roman Empire can scarcely be regarded as unconditionally binding on all Local Churches. In ancient times there were no such districts in the Churches of Alexandria and Rome, and in a later age, as an intermediate stage between dioceses and the central administration, they disappeared for the most part from the structure of Local Orthodox Churches. As for the mixed composition of the Council, made up partly of appointed bishops and partly of bishops chosen by election, it is impossible to find any reference to this in the ancient canons. It is evident that this plan represents a certain free adaptation to the conditions of life in the Russian Church of that time. Nevertheless the article is an expression of the basic idea that bishops must be placed at the head of the Church's administration, and that a Bishops' Council should be independent of secular power in the making of its decisions.

None of these proposals for the reformation of the organization of ecclesiastical life, including the proposals for the creation of Metropolitan districts, got beyond the stage of theoretical discussion.

Though widely criticized, the synodal system remained unaltered. The widespread movement for change took on urgent force, however, in the latter part of the nineteenth century, and the ideas of the Slavophiles played a large role in this movement. Their ideas included: a view of the Church as a kind of spiritual organism, founded on the free unity of all its members with respect to one another and also to the divine Head of the Church, a unity devoid of all constraint; a concept of the conciliarity of the Church's life and of the freedom of the human spirit; and a distinction between the "land" and the State. Such ideas tended to strengthen the protest against the transformation of the Church into an institution of the State set under an Ober-Procurator, as "Head of the Department of Orthodox Church Affairs." They also clarified and gave form to the notion of the direct participation not only of bishops but also of the lower clergy and the whole people of the Church in the ordering of ecclesiastical life. Such a concept of the role of the people was reflected also in the Encyclical Letter of the Eastern Patriarchs to the Roman Pope in 1848, in which it is said that "neither the hierarchy nor councils could ever introduce novelty, since with us the guardian of piety and faith is the very Body of the Church, i.e., the people themselves." (Art. 17).

Two points of view are encountered in the ecclesiastical movements which began to take shape in the opening years of the twentieth century: first, the idea of the exclusively episcopal administration of the Church; and second, the concept of the participation of all the people of the Church in the ordering of ecclesiastical affairs.

III

The Role of the Holy Synod in the Restoration of Conciliarity

THE BEGINNING of the twentieth century was marked by attempts to bring about a genuine reorganization of the synodal system. The initiative in these efforts came now from the Holy Synod itself.

On December 12th, 1904, an Imperial Ukaz was published, setting forth a series of reforms in State administration, among them the abolition of certain restrictions on religious freedom. This was bound to improve the legal position of non-Orthodox communities. The Orthodox Church felt that it had been overlooked. In the era of freedom of conscience, Orthodoxy could find itself in more difficult circumstances than other confessions. The spokesman for the traditional policies of the Orthodox Church at this time was the President of the Holy Synod, Metropolitan Antony (Vladkovsky) of St. Petersburg, who was held in high esteem by Emperor Nicolas II. Metropolitan Antony was wise enough to take leadership in the movement for ecclesiastical reform which was then in full flood, and to direct it along proper channels.

The difficult task of by-passing the all-powerful Ober-Procurator K. P. Pobedonostsev was made easier by the support of the President of the Committee of Ministers, S. Yu. Witte. Metropolitan Antony and the Assistant Ober-Procurator V. K. Sabler were invited by Witte to attend the meetings of a Special Conference under the Committee of Ministers called to consider ways of implementing the Ukaz on religious tolerance of December 12th, 1904. While approving the relief being granted to the sects and other major religious communities, Metropolitan Antony pointed out that the Orthodox Church was not being given the same benefit, nor did it have the autonomy now being allowed to these other communities. All this really placed it in an inferior position. Various members of the Special Conference supported the Metropolitan on this point, including its President, S. Yu. Witte. After several days he notified Metropolitan Antony that he had received permission from the Emperor to raise the question of the administrative reform of the Orthodox Church in the Conference, and requested him to make a formal presentation of the desired reforms.

Metropolitan Antony submitted a Memorandum outlining the restrictions layed upon the Church and, in the cautious but precise terms typical of the bureaucratic language of the time, urging the freedom of the Church from its dependence on the State. Proposed changes in ecclesiastical organization were described for the most part in general terms, and only in certain points did he make concrete suggestions. The Metropolitan said that "the excessively vigilant control of the secular power" over ecclesiastical life "was depriving the Church of its autonomy and initiative," that it had — and this was specially emphasized — "limited the Church's sphere of competence almost wholly to worship and the conduct of religious ceremonies," and as a result "was making the Church's voice go completely unheard in both private and public life." The Metropolitan's basic wish was that the Church should be given greater "freedom in the administration of its internal affairs." This freedom was understood in the Memorandum in the sense that the Church should be "freed from any direct State or political mission," so that in its internal affairs "it could be guided mainly by ecclesiastical canons and the moral and religious needs of its members." It was argued in the Memorandum that such a removal of the hand of the State from the Church's internal life ought to be desirable even from the viewpoint of the State itself, since "with its renewed moral authority" the Church could then be "a steadfast supporter of the Orthodox State." The point of the Memorandum was that once the autonomy of the Church was granted, any change in ecclesiastical organization would then have to be regarded as its own internal affair, as something only the Church itself was in a position to determine. Another matter was the re-structuring of the administrative institutions of the State so that they would include representatives of the Church. Such reforms would depend first of all, of course, on the Emperor himself, and it is of these things that Metropolitan Antony speaks in some detail in his Memorandum. He touches especially on such matters as: the granting to the parish of the rights of a legal person (corporation); the inclusion of clergy in local county (zemstvo) institutions — with the parish defined as a lower unit of the county; the granting to the hierarchy of the right to take part in the highest institutions of the State — such as the Council of State or the Committee of Ministers (thus opening up the possibility of escaping the firm grasp of the Ober-Procurator). The Memorandum deals also, in summary fashion, with the revival and renewal of the parish, the decentralization of ecclesiastical administration, the broad-

13

ening of the powers of diocesan conventions with the inclusion in them of lay delegates from the parishes, and with the reform of the ecclesiastical courts. There is no direct mention of the calling of a Church Council (Sobor) or of its composition. The main emphasis of the Memorandum in this matter is: "Should not His Imperial Majesty be informed at this time of the urgent need for the arrangement of a special conference of representatives of the Church's hierarchy, with the participation of competent persons from the clergy and laity," so that a plan might be drafted for the necessary changes and reforms in ecclesiastical administration. There is no mention whatever of any sort of representation of the Government in such a conference.[8]

Metropolitan Antony was continuing the policy of Metropolitan Filaret, which was to try to place ecclesiastical matters in ecclesiastical hands and to keep the secular power as far away from the internal affairs of the Church as possible. He simply widened the circle of persons called upon to prepare the ecclesiastical reform by admitting the participation of "competent" representatives of the clergy and laity.

Metropolitan Antony's Memorandum evidently struck Witte as being rather dull and failing to give an adequate picture of the needed reforms. Whatever there was in the Metropolitan's report that stemmed from a desire to protect the dignity and independence of the Church was regarded by Witte as a sign of exaggerated caution. Witte received the Memorandum, and then commissioned several liberal professors of the Theological Academies and other prominent people in the Church to develop a concrete plan for the reformation of ecclesiastical administration. On the basis of this work he then had another Memorandum prepared, *O sovremennom polozhenii Pravoslavnoy Tserkvi* ("The Position of the Orthodox Church Today"), which was subsequently presented in his own name, as President of the Committee of Ministers, at the Special Conference on Ecclesiastical Affairs under the Committee of Ministers.[9] This document is significant as the first open attempt by the head of the Government under the Russian Emperor to aid the Church in its struggle for independence. It is an official refutation of the idea of Peter's Ecclesiastical Reglement, a kind of Anti-Reglement.

Witte's Memorandum condemns the basic goal of Peter's reform, which was to reduce the Church to the level of one among several administrative institutions of the State, called to serve the State's interests. "But nothing could be more harmful to the State," the Memorandum asserts, "than to obstruct the development and free manifestation" of the Orthodox faith, this "great force among the people, by trying, as we do now, to press it into the framework of dry bureaucratic principles." The creation of the "Department of Orthodox Church Affairs," with its Ober-Procurator, is seen here as a direct violation of the conciliar principle established by the Church's canon, a violation which has changed the whole spirit of ecclesiastical life. The Holy Synod is declared to be unlawful. Furthermore, the secular and bureaucratic character of the synodal administration is recognized as a barrier between the Church and the people. As a result of all this the Russian Orthodox Church has been "in a state of paralysis" since the time of Peter the Great. The reasons for the alienation of society from the Church are rooted, according to the Memorandum, not just in religious indifferentism and the pagan character of secular culture, but also "in the very style of ecclesiastical life, congealed and cut off from the interests which are now stirring society."

Although in content Witte's Memorandum implied a sweeping rejection of Peter's Ecclesiastical Reglement, it had the same general approach to ecclesiastical problems. Once again, the secular power was assuming leadership in a purely ecclesiastical reform, only this time sheltering under references to the Church's canons. The Memorandum sets forth a detailed plan of reforms touching every aspect of the Church's life. Above all it stresses the need to restore conciliarity and the unity of all the living powers of the Church. The proposed reform "must not be the work of government clerks, nor must it be the work of the Synod of Bishops, or even a somewhat larger number of bishops meeting in a Bishops' Council, but rather the task of the whole Russian Church working without outside interference." The Memorandum does away not only with the Ober-Procurator, but also with the exclusive authority of the bishops in Council. "If the Council is to be in fact the voice of the whole Russian Church, it cannot be simply an episcopal college, which is itself an uncanonical institution. Neither ecumenical nor local councils were colleges of prelate-bishops, but assemblies of all the best forces of the Church—from the laity as well as from the clerical orders. Not only priests, but also deacons and simple laymen attended them and took part in their work. "Even the Russian Synod," the Memorandum continues, "originally included representatives of the white clergy as well as bishops, and only over a period of time did it turn into an exclusively episcopal college." The Memorandum goes on to deal in some detail with the means of reviving parish life, with the granting to ecclesiastical organizations of the rights of a juristic person, with the election of clergy, with the organization of "diocesan conventions" as a form of local council, with the reform of ecclesiastical schools. All this is presented with quotations from ecclesiastical journals and citations of particular scholars — especially Prof.

15

N. A. Zaozersky. How all these measures were to be brought into being was not indicated, but the matter was being submitted, obviously, before a secular institution of the State, the Special Conference under the Committee of Ministers.

The Memorandum was a well-intentioned collection of such proposals for ecclesiastical reform as had appeared thus far in Church and secular publications. It reflected the mood of a great many people and groups in the Church. It cannot be said, however, that all of the provisions advanced in the Memorandum were canonically accurate or entirely beyond dispute.

Although Witte was President of the highest organ of the Government, he was unable to carry out the work of reform which he began. The Ober-Procurator of the Holy Synod, K. P. Pobedonostsev, began to do everything possible to restore his own wavering influence. Citing the need for independence in ecclesiastical administration, he insisted before the Emperor that the question of Church reform be transferred from the Special Conference under the Committee of Ministers to the Holy Synod, where he would be able to take it into his own hands. As the newspaper *Kievskoe Slovo* noted in its issue No. 6189 of 1905, it began to appear as if the Church, with its petition to the secular power for the restoration of its rightful autonomy, was being opposed by the Ober-Procurator of the Synod who, in the name of the autonomy of the Church, was asking that this petition be refused.[10]

But here the members of the Synod decided to act independently of the Ober-Procurator. Metropolitan Antony knew that the Emperor himself was very interested in the question of the conciliar government of the Church.[11] The Synod found support not only in individual members of the Government, but also in broad segments of the white clergy and the laity.

A session of the Synod had been called on March 15, 1905, to discuss the question of changes in ecclesiastical organization. Shortly before this session a group of thirty-two priests in St. Petersburg presented to Metropolitan Antony a memorandum on "The urgent need for the restoration of canonical freedom to the Orthodox Church in Russia," with an accompanying letter of petition to the President of the Synod.[12] The memorandum was in part a reflection of the findings of earlier meetings of this group with the Metropolitan himself.

A rather wordy document, evidently composed hastily in the midst of the turmoil and ecclesiastical events, the Memorandum defined a series of major problems in the Church's life, and in particular stressed the idea of the Church as having a function within and in behalf of society. Here was an expression of anguish over the isolation of the Church from public life and social issues which had come as a result of the close association of the

16

Church with the existing regime. "More and more frequently we are hearing reproaches and accusations directed against the Orthodox Church for having allowed social life to pass out of its control . . . so that the creative elements of social life shun the Church, finding it no courageous witness on behalf of social justice, no fearless confession of the truth before men of high as well as low estate." "It is urgently necessary that the Church regain the full power of its beneficial influence on all aspects of human life." Since the shift from serving the interests of the State to service in the interests of society as a whole would be possible only by way of "the freedom of the Church," the Memorandum proposes that the following measures be taken for the restoration of this freedom: the periodic convening of Church Councils under the presidency of the Archbishop of the Imperial city; the election by the Council of a "Sacred" or "Holy" Synod; the formation of district Metropolitan Councils; a reduction of the size of dioceses; election of bishops by clergy and people; the organization of diocesan administration on the principles of conciliarity; and the development of much greater independence of parishes.

The central point of the Petition accompanying the Memorandum to Metropolitan Antony was a "fervent request" that he "use all his influence" to bring about "the summons of a Church Council, at which the bishops, as well as pastors freely elected from every diocese and also representatives of the laity, could consider the present position of the Church from all sides and make decisions on the most urgently pressing ecclesiastical questions." Like the Memorandum prepared by Witte, the Petition of the thirty-two priests extends the composition of the Council beyond that of a purely episcopal college to include both clergy and laity. In the group's Memorandum itself, however, a Local Council of the Russian Church is simply mentioned without any definition of its make-up. After sympathetically accepting the Memorandum of the thirty-two clergy, Metropolitan Antony approved its publication.[13] The accompanying Petition, however, with its definition of the composition of the Council, was not allowed to be published at the same time as the Memorandum.

The Holy Synod met to consider questions concerning the reorganization of ecclesiastical administration on the 15th, 18th and 22nd of March, 1905. K. P. Pobedonostsev sent as his personal representative to these meetings the Assistant Ober-Procurator, V. K. Sabler. The Synod resolved to turn to the Emperor with a request to restore conciliarity in the Russian Church and to summon, according to the canons, a Local Council of Bishops, under the presidency of a Metropolitan or Patriarch. This was a request therefore, not only for the convocation of a Council, but also for the Restoration of the

Patriarchate. Moreover, it was implied that the Council was to be strictly episcopal, with no participation whatever of lower clergy or laity. Sabler is reported to have listened to the speeches of the members of the Synod with an expression of sympathetic concern.[14]

They did not have to wait long for a reply. It came after eight days, on March 31st, 1905. The Ober-Procurator reported that the Emperor did not consider it possible to summon a Council in the alarming current situation, but expressed a readiness "to carry forward this great task ... when a more favorable occasion for such action is presented." (*Tserkovny Vestnik* No. 14, 1905, p. 434).

Pobedonostsev was powerless to stop the matter in the Synod, but evidently still knew how to postpone its realization indefinitely.

It would be wrong, however, to minimize the importance of the imperial resolution of March 31st, 1905. For the first time the synodal organization introduced by Peter the Great was admitted by the Emperor himself to be subject to change. For the first time the need to replace it with a conciliar organization was admitted by Imperial authority. The protracted ecclesiastical and social struggle against the power over the Church held by the Ober-Procurator had ended with moral victory. Condemned by Imperial authority itself, the synodal system could continue now only as an institution doomed to extinction.

The Ober-Procurator felt compelled to propose to the Synod that it make an inquiry among the bishops concerning desired reforms in the Russian Church. Under a decree of the Holy Synod dated July 27th, 1905, there was sent out to all diocesan bishops certain "points under question" in a questionnaire prepared by Pobedonostsev. Replies were to be returned by December of the same year.

IV

The Political Disturbances of 1905 and the Question of a Council

IN THE STRAINED ATMOSPHERE which existed in Russia at the time, partly as a result of the unsuccessful war in the Far East and partly as a result of the growing feeling that promised reforms would never come, this admission by the Tsar of the need for a Local Council with the simultaneous refusal to summon it had the effect not of calming but of sharpening the struggle for conciliarity in the Church. The subject of a Council and of its composition began to be heatedly discussed not only in theological journals but also in the general press, and became more and more deeply rooted in the public mind.

A lively journalistic debate was touched off by the appearance of the "Memorandum of the Thirty-Two." Some welcomed it as the glad ringing of church-bells on a festal day, others regarded it as the ringing of an alarm, as a "violation of discipline." It must be acknowledged, however, that the polemic against it in newspapers and journals was due partially to a misunderstanding. The authors of the Memorandum were criticized, among other things, for not having indicated clearly enough the role of the laity in ecclesiastical life and especially in the Local Council; for being inclined to identify the Church with the clergy; and for apparently having in view the self-government not of the Church but of the hierarchy, with a resulting strengthening of the power of the monks and their ascetic ideal. It was not difficult for one of the thirty-two — Father G. Petrov — to answer this by saying that the Petition of those who drafted the Memorandum was in fact a call for a Council of representatives of all members of the Church: bishops, white clergy and laity, and that this position had been put forward in the Petition to the Metropolitan which had not been cleared for publication, but printed later as a supplement. The Memorandum, of course, had mentioned the Council only in very general terms. (*Russkoe Slovo*, No. 87, 1905).[15]

However, the critics of this Memorandum had touched questions which could not be treated properly without going into more detail. The authors of the first Memorandum therefore presented a second paper to Metropolitan Antony in May of 1905, dealing especially with the composition of a Church Council. The Metropolitan found it impossible to receive it as he had the first. He gave permission, however, to publish it in the form of a separate article.[16] A split was beginning to develop between the views of the Synod and particular groups of the white clergy.

Opposing the episcopal Council projected by the Synod, the second Memorandum of the Thirty-Two defended an "All Church Council" attended not only by bishops but also by elected representatives of the clergy and laity. From the viewpoint of its authors this form of Council expressed the inner unity of the Church and was the characteristic mark of Orthodoxy, distinguishing it from both Roman Catholicism and Protestantism. Catholicism, they said, reduces the Church to the activity of the episcopate. Protestantism, on the other hand, has found itself compelled to reject the hierarchical principle completely. In Orthodoxy the Church is composed of bishops and people together.

19

Archbishop Antony (Khrapovitsky) of Volhynia became the spokesman of the opposing view. He defended the exclusively episcopal membership of a Council. His "Answering Statement" in response to the second Memorandum of the Thirty-Two was addressed directly to the Most Holy Ruling Synod. It was published in the December, 1905, issue of *Bogoslovsky Vestnik* (Theological Messenger). Sharply criticizing this Memorandum and calling its authors "ecclesiastical republicans" and "decadents," Archbishop Antony presented so many weighty canonical notes to support his position[17] that the authors of the Memorandum were forced to clarify their position. About this same time the Group of the Thirty-Two began to broaden its membership. New persons joined the original circle, including prominent persons in the secular world as well as members of the clergy. The group began to consider not just the main questions of ecclesiastical organization, but also "the ways and means of bringing about a Christian society." It asked one of its members, Nicolai Petrovich Aksakov, to compose an answer to Archbishop Antony's Statement. This reply, under the title "The All Church Council and the principle of election in the Church," also appeared in the December issue of *Bogoslovsky Vestnik,* and was later printed as a separate publication.[18] In an effort to give a better foundation to their argument, Aksakov brought much more material from Scripture, canons and history into this article than is to be found in the previous (second) Memorandum.

The polemic on the question of ecclesiastical organization in 1905-1906 produced a whole series of interesting articles devoted to canonical problems. The various points of view expressed on the Council and the rights of its members were to find detailed expression later in the opinions of the members of the Pre-Council Committee (about which we shall speak in the following chapter).

The sudden appearance of theological debate at the heart of Russia's social and political life occurred at the time of the revolutionary explosion. The ecclesiastical question now entered an unexpected new phase. By the Manifesto of October 17th, 1905, the absolute monarchy in Russia came to an end, being replaced by a constitutional monarchy. The Committee of Ministers was replaced by a Council of Ministers with a new membership. The dismissal of K. P. Pobedonostsev came several days after the publication of the Manifesto. Under these new circumstances the time for the summoning of a Council seemed to be near. The replies of the diocesan bishops to the questionnaire sent out by the Synod were now being quickly returned. They indicated how keenly the majority of ruling bishops felt the need for a reform in the general direction of conciliarity, though there were wide divergencies in the details of proposed forms of conciliar administration.

Finally, as a parallel to the Manifesto of October 17th on the summons of a State Duma, a personal rescript of Emperor Nicolas II was issued on December 27, 1905, in the name of Metropolitan Antony of Petersburg, which once more placed the long-postponed Church Council on the agenda. The Emperor expressed his wish "that certain reforms in the organization of the Church be undertaken, on the firm principles of the ecumenical canons," leaving it to the three Metropolitans to fix the exact time for the Council so long awaited by all the faithful sons of the Church. As a Christmas gift the Orthodox Church was at last promised a new conciliar organization. The Holy Synod decided to take the preliminary development of the projected reform into its own hands and not leave it to governmental authorities; all the more so since the latter were at that time far too occupied with urgent political questions. The Synod decided to form a special Pre-Council Committee for the preparation of drafts of new ecclesiastical laws. On January 14, 1906, the Emperor ratified the decision to establish a Pre-Council Committee, and by March 8th of the same year it had begun its work.

Thanks to the wise steps taken by the President of the Synod at that time, Metropolitan Antony, the Pre-Council Committee was a kind of "All Church assembly." The Synod invited representatives of all levels in the Church's life to participate in this Committee. The bishops, twelve in number, were actually in a minority. Besides the bishops there were eight archpriests, nine laymen (known for their contributions to the life of the Church), and about twenty-five professors from the Theological Academies and Universities (of these four were in clerical orders). The professors were indeed in the majority. Representatives of all the major schools of thought in the Church were included. Side by side with Archbishop Antony Khrapovitsky sat his literary adversary N. P. Aksakov, the man who had written in defense of the Group of Thirty-Two. For the first time in the history of the Russian Church its reform was being considered by a committee competent in the realms of ecclesiastical law and history. Only the extraordinary preparedness of the members of this Committee can explain the fact that within ten months it succeeded in developing a whole series of major and significant proposals for the reorganization of the Church.

V

The Pre-Council Committee of 1906 and Its Majority Opinion

EMPEROR NICOLAS' rescript, which appeared in the name of Metropolitan Antony, expressed a wish that "reforms" in the organization of the Russian

Church should be "effected on the firm principles of the ecumenical canons, for the greater consolidation of Orthodoxy." The work of the Pre-Council Committee was indeed carried on in a spirit of faithfulness to the canons accepted by the Ecumenical Councils, that is, to the canons of the Seven Ecumenical Councils, the eight Local Councils, and to the twelve Holy Fathers and others included in the ancient canonical collections of the Orthodox Church. But the Committee's effort to base its work on a strictly formal application of the canons of the fourth through the ninth centuries presented real difficulties, because in the long period since the ninth century there could not fail to be changes in the general conditions of ecclesiastical life, while within the Russian Church itself certain institutions had appeared which were in no sense foreseen by those early canons. "I shall never insist that the institution of vicar bishops is strictly canonical," said Prof. N. N. Glubokovsky, "since it is nowhere directly confirmed or sanctioned by the canons. On the other hand I definitely cannot agree with those who are inclined to the opinion that this is an essentially anti-canonical institution." In Glubokovsky's opinion this institution arose "simply as a result of the inescapable needs of the Church."[19] It should be added here that it is really an exaggeration to speak of the anti-canonical nature of vicar bishops, since in fact they appeared as a modified form of the ancient *chorepiscopoi* (village bishops), preserving the basic characteristics of this earlier institution but adapting them to the demands of a later time.

Archbishop Dimitry of Kherson strongly objected to any attempt to adhere indiscriminately to the letter of all the canons. "Can we really accept the statement made here," he said at one of the meetings, "this life-killing statement, that 'the conditions of life must yield before the demands of the canons.'? What we must be concerned about," he went on, "is not that canons which define in detail certain non-essential aspects of ecclesiastical life, under particular external conditions that existed more than a thousand years ago, should again be observed literally, but that the organizational structure of our Church should be in harmony with what is essential in the canons, and should not in any way directly contradict them." "We must hold to what is essential and basic in the canons, but the details can be accepted by the Church as they fit the circumstances of life . . . It must be remembered also that no man can change the canons for himself in the light of his own judgment. This is a right which belongs to ecclesiastical authority, acting with all due deliberation."

These words focused attention on a very important and difficult task: that of distinguishing the "basic canons" which, "resting on the command of Christ and the teaching of the Apostles, reflect the very essence of the

Church's life" and are not subject to change.[20] But a fulfillment of this task cannot mean the wholesale rejection or alteration of those canons which from one's own standpoint "define only the non-essential aspects of ecclesiastical life." On the contrary, it requires a painstaking research to see exactly which canons were published under conditions which no longer obtain, or have been so radically changed that the canons are not applicable to the present situation. The work of defining this complex of canons still in force involves identifying canons which have lost their force in full or in part either as a result of having been revoked by other canons accepted by the Ecumenical Councils, or because they have been made ineffective by subsequent ecclesiastical practice. Such an approach makes way also for the restoration of some former canonical institutions whenever conditions are again created similar to those existing at the time when such institutions came into being. It leads also to the conclusion that ancient institutions can be changed and adapted to new conditions of life while preserving the principles of ecclesiastical organization which they express. In all this we begin to see the possibility of the further development of Orthodox canon law.

One of the basic subjects discussed by the Pre-Council Committee was the question of the membership of the projected Council, including the question of members' rights. The discussion naturally revolved about the double question whether or not the clergy (priest and deacons) and laity could take part in the Council alongside the bishops, and if (in such a case) they could have equal rights with the bishops in the meetings of the Council.

A majority of the members of the Committee felt that the clergy and laity could attend the Council but could have no decisive vote. Those who defended this view sought support for it, first of all, in the canons. Archbishop Antony (Khrapovitsky) held that in ancient times "only bishops attended the Councils, usually having a Patriarch at their head."[21] According to Prof. N. S. Suvorov one would find nothing in the canons included in the *Kniga Pravil* (Book of Regulations) to indicate the full participation in Council of anyone but bishops, since only bishops were actually members of the Ecumenical Councils. Archimandrites and priests attended only as representatives of absent bishops, and only by their direct commission. Individuals from the ranks of the clergy and laity took part in these Councils only as experts, giving information needed in the matters under consideration.[22]

Grounds for the defense of this position were also sought in ecclesiastical practice. While supporting Prof. Suvorov's assertion that there were no persons from the ranks of the clergy or laity at the Ecumenical Councils as members having full voting rights, Prof. I. S. Berdnikov of the Theological

Academy of Kazan pointed out also that representatives of the clergy and laity did in fact attend, not only the Apostolic Council in Jerusalem, but also, in the post-apostolic period, several Local Councils in the second and third centuries. He showed that according to the records of the Council of Carthage in 257 A.D. there were present eighty-seven bishops, as well as a large number of presbyters and deacons, and a greater part of the people. There is also mention, he said, of clergy and laity at Councils in the fourth, fifth and sixth centuries, although the total number of such Local and Diocesan Councils is extremely small. "What is important, however," said Professor Berdnikov, "is not the mere fact that there were occasions when the clergy and laity were permitted to attend a Council, but the significance of their presence at these Councils." We may learn something, in his opinion, from the very picture we get of these meetings, as described, for example, by Prof. A. P. Lebedev in his book *Ob uchastii miryan na soborakh* ("The Participation of the Laity in Church Councils," Moscow, 1906, p. 17). On the basis of a number of early descriptions of particular Local Councils, Lebedev was able to give a general view of the way business was carried on at these assemblies. The picture we have is one of bishops sitting in a semicircle in the middle of the church, with the presbyters occupying places behind them, while the deacons stand around their bishops, and the laity stand also. All persons present could take part in the deliberations. Once a matter had been fully considered, the president would put the question to a vote of the bishops. Their decision was then declared to all the people present in the assembly, who would express their agreement with the decision by acclamations. Lebedev's description was thus in full harmony with the opinion already advanced in earlier theological literature, that is, that "the decisive vote at Councils in ancient times belonged to the bishops alone — all the rest, presbyters, deacons, confessors and the faithful had a consultative vote only."[23]

In the eyes of its supporters this view found confirmation in the actual position of the clergy and laity in the Orthodox Church. In the words of S. T. Golubev of the Kiev Academy, "The Orthodox Church does not regard the laity as Catholicism does, as an inert mass moved toward the gates of Paradise by the Church's hierarchy. It considers the participation of the laity in ecclesiastical affairs as lawful, flowing out of the spirit of the Orthodox doctrine, and therefore always to be desired. Thus also the Orthodox Church (and here is a fundamental difference between Orthodoxy and Protestantism) assigns a particular realm of activity, and particular limits within this realm, for the participation of the laity, as the ecclesiastical canons show."[24] These "limits" for the living and active participation of the laity in the Church's life are determined by the "hierarchical structure" of the Church, which obliges us to recognize a position of subordination for some and privileges for others.

The superior privileges of the hierarchy and clergy do not, of course, completely prohibit the laity from exercising their lesser privileges in their own sphere of action. The problem of the position of the laity in the Church is precisely the problem of defining the proper limits of their activity. There was no full agreement on this point among the supporters of the consultative function of the laity in a Council. Prof. M. A. Ostroumov of the University of Kharkov held that "the laity have only the right to a Christian religious education, to Christian sanctification in the Sacraments, and to guidance by their pastors." The active role of the laity was thus reduced to a simple obedience to the guidance of pastors, and the receiving from them of the gifts of Divine grace. The laity are, as Prof. Ostroumov himself put it, in the position of "persons under authority." By thus reducing the active role of the laity in the Church to the level of passive obedience (in the Catholic manner, according to Prof. Golubev), Ostroumov was unable to find any real basis for allowing them to attend a Council. "By what right," he asks, "can the laity, who are canonically not called to the hierarchical office, take part in a Council? How can those who are under authority participate in authority? They have no right to this whatever, nor can they have, since this would contradict the very concept of one placed under authority. The right to participate in Councils cannot be derived from the fact that the laity are members of the Church, since from this fact we derive only the concept of their submission to authority." In spite of all this, however, Ostroumov agreed with the idea that laymen should be permitted to attend the Council... but on the grounds of "ecclesiastical economy" (permitted deviation from the exact implementation of ecclesiastical laws), out of a "condescension to human need and a love of mankind."[26] His reference to "economy," however, could do nothing to soften the contradictory nature of his position. An exception to the requirements of common canonical norms on the principle of ecclesiastical "economy" can be granted lawfully by supreme ecclesiastical authority only, to separate individuals or groups and under such circumstances, unforeseen by the law, as would render the strict observance of the general norms contrary to the interests of the Church or to the task of saving individual men. While granting the dispensation or exception from the general rule, the rule itself remains in force for the rest of the Church. But the admission of the laity to a Council "by economy" creates a general rule which has the effect of abrogating and replacing the basic canonical principle, advanced by Ostroumov himself, which prohibits them from becoming members of a Council. The laity thus receive rights which, in his own words, "they neither do nor can possess." Needless to say, "economy" cannot go quite as far as that. New law cannot be created by way of "economy."

Other supporters of the admission of clergy and laity to the Council would allow them a much greater and more significant role in ecclesiastical life. In his "Response" to the questionnaire of the Holy Synod Bishop Stefan of Mogilyev had written: "Realization of the principle of conciliarity, as the broad interaction and living communion of all members of the Church's organism, requires a regular and organized representation of the laity."[27] Bishop Stefan defended this position also in the meetings of the Pre-Council Committee. Metropolitan Antony of St. Petersburg was another who saw the Church as the unity of all the faithful. He too opposed Ostroumov, saying that the very fact that clergy and laity are numbered as members of the Church is enough to show that they are in a position to be members of a Council. "We all know," he said, "that the Church consists of bishops, clergy and laity, forming as it were a coherent whole. It is on this basis that the participation in a Council not only of bishops but also of clergy and laity has been acknowledged desirable."[28] But the Metropolitan emphasized the need to distinguish in the Church between pastors and flock and between bishops and priests, and he made it clear that the granting of equal right to bishops, priests and laity would be "a violation of the fundamental principles of ecclesiastical life," since "the fulness of ecclesiastical powers resides in the episcopate."[29] Thus he fully accepted the notion of the participation of the clergy and laity in a consulting role.

When Archbishop Antony (Khrapovitsky) of Volhynia reminded Metropolitan Antony that the Holy Synod had petitioned the Sovereign for the summons of a Council of bishops only, the Metropolitan "explained that the petition had not come from the initiative of the Synod itself, but had been inspired by the course of historical events." At any rate, he said, "from the responses of the Diocesan Bishops, the desirability of inviting the clergy and laity to take part in the Council has been made plain."[30] Archbishop Antony of Volhynia remained the sole unwavering opponent of the participation of the clergy and laity in the Council, granting only that laymen could appear at the Council as petitioners to set forth their desires and needs.[31]

VI

A Minority Opinion in the Pre-Council Committee

W<small>HILE</small> most of the members of the Committee held that the decisive vote in the Council should be reserved to the bishops, a minority vigorously defended the equal voting rights of all members of the Council and the right of the clergy and laity to participate on a par with the bishops in the consideration and deciding of all questions. This small but energetic group included Archpriest P. Ya. Svetlov, a professor of Kiev University, Father A. P. Rozhdestvensky, a professor of the Theological Academy of St. Petersburg, Prof. V. Z. Zavitnevich of the Theological Academy of Kiev, Prof. V. I. Nesmelov of the Theological Academy of Kazan, Professor M. N. Mashanov of the same Academy, and N. P. Aksakov. On a number of questions this group was joined by N. D. Kuznetsov, as well as others. Their view included the doctrine of the Church as a spiritual or moral unity, and the juridical consequences deriving from this concept.

Some members of this group acknowledged that "the canons actually give no indication whatever of the necessity for the participation of presbyters and laity in a Council." This did not disturb them, however. "It must be proved," said Aksakov, "that the canons prohibit such participation."[32] In supporting this view, N. D. Kuznetsov pointed out a possible conclusion to be drawn from it: "The concepts of decisive and consultative votes at a Council are alien to the history of the Church and to the very canons which many people would like to use to resolve all the questions put to us by life. Here, of course, we come up against the need to be guided not by such concepts as these, but by the general principles contained in the doctrine of the Church."[33]

In a paper entitled "A separate opinion of a minority group on the question of the composition of the Council," we have an expression and special interpretation of the "canonical basis" which this minority group, as well as the entire Pre-Council Committee, sought so vigorously to maintain, and also its view of the Church. According to this paper those things are "canonical" which correspond "to the highest plan of ecclesiastical life, to that unattainable ideal which has never in any place been fully realized in the whole wealth of its content, but which has always sought out concrete forms of realization more or less closely corresponding to its ideal norms. The ideal is eternal, the forms are changing. . . reflecting the changeableness of this constantly evolving life." It was in the light of this understanding of what is canonical that the supporters of this view insisted "that the forthcoming reforms of our Church must be carried out in the spirit of the canonical principles of the ancient Ecumenical Church." On the same grounds they refused to admit "the notion that the reforms of our times must inevitably be a mechanical reproduction of old historical patterns, very possibly unsuitable for our times." The long expected reforms must be not "a simple mechanical reproduction of old models, but the renewal of the Church on the foundation of its inner and primary principles." In any study of historical forms, "it is necessary to look for the eternal principles of life which manifest themselves in these forms." These primary foundations and eternal principles are engraved above all, according to the "Separate Opinion" of the minority group, in the Word of God, in particular in the doctrine of the Church as the Body of Christ and the account of the Apostolic Council of Jerusalem.

"In calling the Church the Body of Christ," the minority said, "St. Paul makes very clear, on the one hand, the close inner bond that must exist between the members of the Church, and on the other hand, the deep significance that each individual member has in the Church as Christ's Body. (ROM. 12:1-5; I COR. 12:12-27; EPH. 4:1-32). At the same time the Apostle warns that no one member should exalt himself above the others (ROM. 12:3)."[34] "This excludes every striving for an exclusive position in the Church to be gained by pushing others aside," the Separate Opinion continues. "Those members of the body which seem the weakest, according to the Apostle, are the very members that are needed most of all."[35] "The elevation of bishops to a point where they are regarded as the only vital, active members of the Church, and the consequent lowering of others to a point where they are seen as dead, passive members, deals a blow to the organic unity of Christ's Church."[36] "The purpose for which all the members of the Church are united in the one Body of Christ . . . consists in the making perfect of each individual person in the task of love (EPH. 4:15)." "Love. . . is the organic force which unites all the members of Christ's Church in the one Body of Christ, at the same time revealing itself as the foundation on which the conciliar principle in the Church is established."

The Separate Opinion goes on to say: "Mutual love prevailed, of course, in the Apostolic Council in Jerusalem." Here there were "neither superiors nor subordinates, in the juridical sense of these terms; neither persons in authority nor those slavishly subordinated to them. . . Here all were able to speak and persuade others to the measure of their ability and understanding." Apostles, presbyters and the brethren took part in the deliberations of the assembly. The epistle to Antioch was a conciliar act executed by the Apostles, the presbyters and all the brethren of the Church (Acts 15:7, 12, 22, 23, 25). This Council is important as an authoritative standard for the kind of relationship that should exist between members of the Council. "Here all recognize themselves as full and equal members of the one Body of Christ, organically united by the power of love. This is precisely why the decisive vote here belongs not to Apostles, not to presbyters, not to the brethren, taken separately, but to the unanimity of all, since only in such singleness of mind does love appear, the basic law and creative power of the Church of Christ."[37] In the post-apostolic period and in the epoch of the Ecumenical Councils we encounter, according to the Separate Opinion, "this same conciliar principle, although its external expression took different forms, depending on the particular circumstances of each period." The early rule governing the participation of the clergy and laity in Councils became physically impossible with the passage of time, in view of the increase in the number of the faithful. Councils came to be attended by bishops only, the chosen men of the people, enjoying the full trust of the communities which had elected them. "It was for this last reason, and not by virtue of their episcopal office, that the conciliar decrees of the bishops acquired the authority which they possessed in the eyes of believers." Referring to the Epistle of the Eastern Patriarchs, who had accepted "the very Body of Christ, that is, the whole people, as the guardian of piety," the Separate Opinion stresses the point that the binding force of the decisions of episcopal Councils depended on "the whole people of the Church, whose unanimous acceptance was the sole proof of the validity of a conciliar decree."[38]

All these arguments were crowned by yet another, drawn from the same doctrine of the Church as the Body of Christ. The Church is revealed as the Body of Christ insofar as it is the spiritual or ethical unity of the faithful. Canonists look at the Church as a juridical union. "But the juridical approach to questions concerning the rights and mutual relations of the members of the Council is excluded," said the authors of the Separate Opinion, "by the concept of the Church as the Body of Christ. The distinction between a decisive and a consultative vote does not correspond to the nature of the Church as an institution which in its essence is not juridical but ethical, defined by the principle of Christian love and not by the principle of law."[39] Practical arguments were also added to considerations of principle in support of the broad active participation of the laity in the organs of Church administration. Kuznetsov emphasized that "the Orthodox Church considers laymen as reasoning sheep, who in the light of Church history have shown themselves capable not only of giving wise counsel for the good of the Church, but also of taking an active hand in working for the common good." He reminded his listeners also of the "clearly expounded insight of the Apostles, that care for material things should not distract the clergy from the work of pastoral ministry."[40] Prof. Svetlov remarked that in recent years in Russia there had been a clear-cut and urgent demand, not only from the hierarchy but also from the clergy and laity, for an end to the isolation of bishops from their flocks and the restoration of wholeness to the Body of Christ "by an active participation of all in its life and work." He felt that if the All Russian Local Church Council was turned now into a Council of bishops only, it might well drive the best and most vital elements out of the Church. It would be to lose this "unique and golden opportunity to renew the Church on the principle of conciliarity." "A refusal to let the clergy and laity take their place as genuine and fully competent members of the Council," said Svetlov, "would also be a bad omen for the future of the Council itself. It would be discredited in the eyes of the Church, would lose its moral authority, and in the end would have small chance of acceptance by the Church as a whole."[41]

The arguments of the minority group in the Pre-Council Committee were not left unanswered. The Separate Opinion clearly testified to the lively sense its authors had of the spiritual character of the Church and to their appreciation of its sanctity, but it was not difficult for Prof. Berdnikov to expose the extreme vagueness of the "canonical basis" on which the minority proposed to build its ecclesiastical reform, as well as the obscurity of the references to "the inner fundamental principles" from which this "ever youthful Church is constantly renewed." The external structure of the Church should, of course, be in harmony with its "fundamental principles," i.e., with those basic structural elements established and made plain in the Holy Scriptures. But Orthodox canon law, as Prof. Berdnikov pointed out, does in fact place the Holy Scriptures at the basis of all ecclesiastical legislation, at the same time seeking grounds also in tradition and in the accepted usages of the Church. The decrees of the Ecumenical Councils are founded on Holy Scripture and represent the best possible commentary on and exposition of those passages in Scripture which deal with the structure of the Church. To regard all the ecumenical canons as nothing more than temporary and changeable expressions of the eternal truth of the Church means to reject that view of the basis of ecclesiastical organization which has been defined by the Church itself.

It is precisely the canons of the Ecumenical Councils that have determined the organizational structure which has been preserved by the Orthodox Church down to the present time, and by which it may be distinguished from other Christian Churches and communities. Alongside definitions of the constant and basic principles of ecclesiastical organization there are also in this body of law certain decrees of a temporary character. But with each particular decree of this kind it is necessary to demonstrate that it really has for some reason lost its force, either as a result of having been nullified by later canons or ecclesiastical practice, or because of the disappearance of the conditions under which it was originally established. To dismiss canons simply because they are not in harmony with conclusions drawn from Scripture by a given group of churchmen would mean, in the opinion of Berdnikov, to put a "subjective" understanding in the place of ecclesiastical canons. Conclusions drawn from Holy Scripture by particular canonists today are unable to destroy the force of conclusions already defined by earlier Councils of the Church.

The notion of the equality of the voices of bishops, clergy and laity was refuted by a number of members of the Committee, who spoke of the primacy of the episcopate in the Orthodox Church, showing how it is in perfect harmony with Scripture, canon law and tradition. This primacy places the episcopate above the clergy and laity, and safeguards its supreme position by rejecting any higher authority. It is for this reason, the majority said, that the episcopate has the deciding vote not only at strictly episcopal Councils, but also at Councils where clergy and laity are in attendance. Thus at the Council of Carthage in 257 A.D., held under the presidency of St. Cyprian, decisions were made by having each bishop in the Council state his opinion on the question in turn, in spite of the fact that there were present "a great number of presbyters and deacons" and a "greater part of the people." There is reason to believe that even at the Apostolic Council in Jerusalem, "after much debate," the decision was formulated and promulgated by the Apostles, proving that it could not be in any sense contrary to their wishes.

A point which came under particularly heavy fire was the minority view that the doctrine of the Church as the Body of Christ excludes all distinction in the degree of influence different members of the Church might have on ecclesiastical administration, and that this doctrine must inevitably lead to the admission of equal rights for all in a Church Council. The bearing of the concept of the Body of Christ "on the form of the ecclesiastical organism," said Prof. Almazov, "can mean one thing only: that the clergy and laity, as members of the ecclesiastical organism, are necessary to its existence. However their necessity is one thing, while their significance in the administration and essential activity of the organism is quite another matter." In this connection it was emphasized more than once, especially by Archbishop Antony (Khrapovitsky), that a body presupposes many organs with different functions, and that the specialized functions of a particular organ cannot be performed by another. In the view of the majority a correct comparison of the Church with a living organism leads to a conclusion exactly opposite to that of the minority. It leads us to admit a unique significance for each organ in the life of the

Church, each with its own degree of influence, and to reject any full equality among the members of the Church as something contrary to Orthodox canon law.[42]

Prof. Suvorov drew special attention to the fundamental difficulty in using the doctrine of the Body of Christ for a definition of the rights of different members of the Church at a Council. "In general," he said, "no definite conclusions can be drawn from a comparison of the Church with the Body of Christ."[43] He then pointed out the inner contradiction in the minority position. "Those who speak of 'the Body of Christ' and 'the mystical organism of the Church' and at the same time reproach their adversaries for having 'transported concepts borrowed from the juridical realm into the sphere of strictly moral relationship,' are themselves demanding a very definite juridical equality for all members of the Church in the forthcoming Council, in spite of the fact that they are imbued with the idea of the moral relationships existing in the mystical Body of Christ."[44] At the basis of Suvorov's objection lay the thought that it is inadmissible to draw conclusions from things in the mystical, spiritual world as if they referred to the properties of things existing in the altogether different conditions of this earthly world.

The Church on earth stands on the border between two worlds. It belongs to the earthly world insofar as it is a union of people living on earth. But in contrast with other earthly unions, it has in view the creation of a spiritual unity of men with God and the highest spirits of the Heavenly Realm. It pursues goals which go beyond the limits of earthly existence, seeking to make men capable of rising after death to the life of the Kingdom that is to come. The Church was founded not by men, as other earthly unions are, but by the God-Man Jesus Christ and His Apostles. It was placed under the guidance of the episcopate, which derives its authority from Christ through His Apostles. It is enlightened by the teaching of Christ, and endowed with the life-giving gifts of divine grace bestowed in the Sacraments. And only because supernatural powers really do exist in the Church's life is it in a position to fulfill its great task of saving men, that is, of drawing them out of the sin that has laid waste the human organism, and setting them on the true path of life proper to human nature, a life that is not to be realized without communion with God.

As an earthly union, the Church is made up of men, of spiritual-physical beings bound up in their everyday life with the material world. To realize its spiritual goals the earthly Church has need, then, for a certain concrete structure. In order that its holy task can be realized by men moved by sinful inclinations, certain rules of conduct must be established to defend the community of the Church as a whole and also its individual members from the destructive power of their own weaknesses. This requires a proper delineation of the rights and obligations of the Church's members, and the establishment of some practical norms which have been developed over many centuries to insure the successful working of human associations. The mystical life of the Church and God's relationship to men are not to be contained, of course, within the framework of rights and obligations. They lie beyond the limits of ecclesiastical law. But to the extent that the Church is one among other human associations, its activity can be defined by legal norms, which must then be adapted to the carrying out of the Church's special tasks. In defining the structure of the earthly Church one must take into account, therefore, not only its spiritual foundations, but also the conditions of its earthly existence.

As a spiritual unity of believers with Christ, and of one believer with another in Christ, the Church manifests itself as the Body of Christ. This concept is not just a simile or figure of speech. It bears witness to a unity so intimate that it can be said that all the faithful having "one spirit" form "one body"—with Christ at the head (EPH. 4:3-4). But from the words of the Apostle it appears also that the Church as the Body of Christ is still in the process of being built up. To the degree that we are imbued with the spirit of Christ and follow His commandment of love there occurs, in the words of the Apostle, "a building up of the Body of Christ. . . until we all come into the unity of the faith and knowledge of the Son of God. . . to the measure of the full stature of Christ." (EPH. 4:11-13). This building up of the Body of Christ is a real and genuine phenomenon of the spiritual world, not perceived by the physical senses of the body, but keenly felt by the faithful as the blowing of the Spirit of God, as the unceasing manifestation of the Kingdom of the Good—the Kingdom of God. If the process of edifying the Body of Christ within the framework of the Church has not yet been completed, this means that the members of the Church have not yet all been formed in perfect unity with Christ, nor have they entered yet fully into the make-up of His Body. So long as the process of upbuilding the Body goes on, measures must be taken against the human weaknesses which hinder the forward movement of this process.

The complex task of organizing the earthly Church is one of creating a system for uniting people in which the bestowal on them of the gifts of divine grace will be guaranteed, and in which there will be the greatest possibility of realizing perfectly the upbuilding of the Body of Christ in the unity of faith and love. Thus in the Holy Scriptures there is not only the doctrine of the Church as the Body of Christ but also a number of statements by Christ Himself and His Apostles on the subject of the earthly organization of the Church: on the power of the hierarchy to teach and conduct the Sacraments

(MATT. 10:1-15; MATT. 28:19-20; LK. 22:17-20); on the forgiveness of sins (MATT. 18:18; JN. 20:23); on marriage and divorce (MATT. 5:32; 19:3-11; ROM. 7:2-3; I COR. 7:2ff); on the qualities and obligations of sacred ministers (I TIM. 3:1-13; TITUS 1:5-9; I PET. 5:1-9; I COR. 12:28); on complaints against the clergy (I TIM. 5:19); on the treatment of those who have sinned, and on the position of those who have been excluded from the Church by not having heard its voice (MATT. 15-17; I COR. 5:9-15; I TIM. 5:20); even on relationships with civil authority (MATT. 22:17-21; LK. 20:21-25; I PET. 2:13-17; ROM. 13:1-7). The Jerusalem Council presented a model for the resolution of the most important questions in the Church's life. The Fathers of the Ecumenical and ancient Local Councils were men who had grown up under the conditions of Roman law and order and whose minds were deeply influenced by Roman legal concepts. It is not surprising, then, that they brought these ideas into the realm of the Church's life and used some of them for the regulation of relationships within the community of the Church, adapting them to the goals of the Church's activity.

Since the earthly Church belongs at once to the spiritual as well as to the material world, its external organization cannot be derived simply from the concept of the Body of Christ as a purely spiritual unity. Prof. Suvorov's observations dealt a decisive blow to the attempt of the minority to establish the equal rights of the clergy and laity in the Council.

VII

The Regulations of the Pre-Council Committee

THE MINORITY POSITION in determining the question of the composition and rights of members of the Council was rejected. In a General Meeting of the Pre-Council Committee it was decided that the Council should consist of bishops, clergy and laity, the clergy and laity, however, being given only a consultative voice in the work of the Council. They would "participate in the discussion of all matters and questions before the Council," according to the Committee's resolution, "but the definitions and regulations of the Council would be composed and subscribed to by the bishops only." The clergy and laity could also be invited to take part in special commissions, when the Council felt this was necessary. The very cautiously worded resolution of the Committee provided that: "for the preliminary examination of questions formulated by the Council, commissions may be formed, if the Council sees the need, from the membership of the Council, including the clergy and laity as well as bishops. Such commissions will submit their findings to the judgment of the General Assembly of the Council."

Only ruling diocesan bishops are to be members of the Council. Suffragan (vicar) and retired bishops can attend the Council only if invited by the Holy Synod. In connection with the participation of the clergy and laity, the proposal was made several times that the diocesan bishop be permitted to invite whoever he wished to be present with him in the Council's meetings. Metropolitan Antony of St. Petersburg objected to this proposal. He felt that "elections were necessary, in the sense that the bishop himself would wish to know the thinking of his clergy and laity... If he were to select a person whom no one had elected this could lead to scandal and dissention..." He therefore proposed that a number of candidates be elected and the bishop should invite persons to the Council only from among these candidates.[45] In accordance with this suggestion the Pre-Council Committee ruled that candidates for Council membership from the diocese should be elected at deanery meetings, one clergyman and one layman from each deanery, and that from this number the diocesan bishop should then select and approve one representative from the clergy and one from the laity.[46]

The definition of the composition of the Council was in the mind of its authors not only a renewal but also a further development of ancient practice. The early Church knew only direct popular assemblies, in the election of bishops, for example, and was not familiar with representative institutions or the election of Council members. The Pre-Council Committee had introduced into the composition of the Council elected representatives of the clergy and laity from every diocese, with the provision that these representatives be approved by the diocesan bishop. Early documents show that the clergy and laity took part in only a few of the ancient Local Councils. Now their participation was being accepted as a formal and general rule. The ancient order was thus retained, but in a new form, corresponding to the new circumstances of social and public life.

Beside the regulations concerning periodic Councils of the Russian Church, the Pre-Council Committee also made decisions affecting the composition of the Holy Synod, the Patriarch, the procedure for electing diocesan bishops, the reformation of diocesan administration and the ecclesiastical courts, and the establishment of Metropolitan districts. These districts had been regarded earlier as an introduction of self-government in certain areas of the Church's life, and as a step toward the conciliar self-government of the entire Church. Now, with the acceptance of the proposal for a Local Council of the Russian Church, the significance of the Metropolitan districts was diminished, and their formation was admitted to be simply desirable, not obligatory; even then they were to be created only "for pastoral reasons... and not as judicial and administrative institutions."[47]

The sessions of the Pre-Council Committee ended in the middle of December, 1906. On April 25th of the following year the Committee's completed Regulation for the summons of an extraordinary Council of the Russian Church was ratified by the Emperor.

All that remained now was the summons itself.

VIII

The Holy Synod Under the Provisional Government

THE RUSSIAN GOVERNMENT managed to recover somewhat from the revolutionary shock at the end of 1905, and in the following year it set out again on the path of social reforms, although these were undertaken on the most limited scale possible. The first State Duma was dismissed on July 7, 1906, shortly after it had been called. The second State Duma suffered a similar fate on June 3, 1907. The sessions of the Pre-Council Committee were also brought to a close before all the work that had been assigned to it had been completed.

Time passed, but there was no sign of the promised summons of a Council. Metropolitan Antony of St. Petersburg died, and the membership of the Holy Synod was very substantially altered. Five years passed. In order to dispel the impression that the waiting had indeed been in vain, a new "Pre-Council Conference" was formed in 1912, designed to reduce the material of the Pre-Council Committee to a form more suitable for consideration at the Council itself. The Pre-Council Conference did not have the character of a broadly based gathering of representatives of various schools of theological thought as did the Pre-Council Committee of 1906. The reports and findings of the Pre-Council Conference were bound into five bulky volumes. Still the Council was not summoned. The beginning of the World War in 1914 still further removed the time of its calling.

The Council of the Russian Church was convened at last only after the revolution of 1917, during the time of the Provisional Government. The Holy Synod remained under the control of the Ober-Procurator right up to the end of the Imperial Government, although the office was officially condemned. Even under the Provisional Government which emerged after the revolution there was still a tendency to keep the administration of the Church in the hands of the State, and to carry out ecclesiastical reforms by action of civil authority.

The Provisional Government regarded itself as a secular, non-confessional authority, but admitted the need to give special attention to the Orthodox Church as historically the most important Church in Russia, and so it too appointed its Ober-Procurator to the Holy Synod. The man named to this position was V. N. Lvov, for many years a member of the Commission for Ecclesiastical Affairs of the State Duma. At the first meeting of the Holy Synod on March 4th, 1917, the new Ober-Procurator declared in the name of the Provisional Government that the primary task of this Government was the liberation of the Church from its subjection to the State. This would be accomplished, he said, by means of a Local Council, which would have the task of organizing the self-government of the Church. Up to that time the Synod must accept the "directives" of the Provisional Government through him, as the Ober-Procurator of the new Government. His words seemed to carry a certain disbelief in the readiness of the members of the Holy Synod to bring about the free self-government of the Church, and suggested also a peculiar desire to force the Church to become free in the form that seemed most desirable to the Government.

To hasten this reforming activity several changes were made in the membership of the episcopate. Two members of the Holy Synod—Metropolitan Pitirim of St. Petersburg and Metropolitan Makary of Moscow—were removed, their appointments having been made apparently under the influence of Rasputin. Metropolitan Vladimir of Kiev became president of the Synod. This somewhat modified Synod then published an Encyclical on the expected summons of an All Russian Local Council, and carried out several reforms in diocesan administration. It also continued to guard its dignity as the highest hierarchical organ of the Church in the face of the "directives" of the secular government. It was not long before relations between Lvov and the members of the Synod became extremely strained. The members of the Synod only very reluctantly accepted the policy of the Provisional Government as laid down by Lvov, a policy that tended to reduce even more the position of the Orthodox Church in the State. In particular they were opposed to the placing of a large number of parochial schools under the authority of the Ministry of Education. The members of the Synod also opposed certain reforms carried out in a way which they considered to be inconsistent with the views of the Church, for example, the question of divorce. They very unwillingly accepted laws dealing with the reform of the upper and intermediate ecclesiastical schools, which had the effect of reducing the right of the central ecclesiastical authority to administer these schools. These disagreements in the question of how to meet the demands of the times were only sharpened by Lvov's tactless manner. An ill-tempered individual, he simply revived the type of authoritarian Ober-Procurator who sees himself as the "commander" of the Holy Synod. If the Synod made a decision which he did not like he would raise his voice and shout: "I will not let this get by!" In this strained atmosphere, during a recess in the meetings of the Synod over the Feast of Easter, Lvov closed down the official publication of the Synod, *Tserkovny Vestnik* ("The Church Messenger"), and without any consideration of the question in a meeting of the Synod he transferred the publication of this journal to another editorial committee, at the Theological Academy of St. Petersburg. He then asked three members of the Synod who had remained in St. Petersburg to endorse by their signatures the acceptance of this decision by the Synod. Two of them subscribed: Sergius, Archbishop of Vladimir (who became Patriarch of Moscow in 1943) and Protopresbyter T. Shavelsky. Tikhon, Archbishop of Vilna (Patriarch of Moscow in 1917-1924) refused to give his signature. In these constantly worsening relations with the Synod, Lvov resorted to dismissing the Synod itself.

Lvov soon named new members to the Synod, including archpriests as well as bishops. Among the clergy appointed were several professors from institutions of higher learning, including A. P. Rozhdestvensky, former member of the minority group of the Pre-Council Committee of 1906. From the membership of the previous Synod there remained only Archbishop Sergius and Platon, former Exarch of Georgia (who later became head of the Russian Church in America). Even with this new membership, however, things went badly. At the outset the new members of the Synod expressed profound regret that they had been called to a weighty and responsible task "solely by the will of the Provisional Government" and not by the choice of their fellow pastors and all the faithful sons of the Church. They indicated that they were remaining in the Synod only in view of the urgent need to reorganize the supreme administrative structure of the Church. Clashes with Lvov continued. Its members held that the Ober-Procurator had no right to take measures independently, without the knowledge and approval of the Holy Synod. The President stated on several occasions, in the name of all members of the Synod, that the desire of the Ober-Procurator to undertake action illegally in a given question would compel them to resign their office, and only in the face of this was he restrained.[48]

The most important action of the new Synod was the formation of a new preparatory commission for the calling of a Council—the Pre-Council Consultation. There were about sixty persons in the Consultation, including bishops, clergy, laity, and not a few professors. As Assistant Ober-Procurator, A. V. Kartashev was also a member. The Synod and the Pre-Council Consultation found themselves working in an atmosphere of renewed ferment in ecclesiastical circles, with the formation of special groups of clergy and laymen seeking ways to revive the Church's life. The work of the Pre-Council Consultation moved forward quickly, taking advantage of materials from the Pre-Council Commitee of 1906 and the Pre-Council Conference of 1912. On the basis of its findings the Synod very quickly published a series of "provisional" decrees: on parish and diocesan administration and on the election of bishops. On July 5th, 1917, the Synod ratified the Regulation on the election of members of the Council passed by the Pre-Council Consultation, and ordered that the Council be convened on August 15th, 1917.[49]

In the meantime during the month of July there were radical changes at the top level of the Provisional Government. A. F. Kerensky became the President of the new Government, in place of Prince G. E. Lvov. V. N. Lvov was obliged to vacate the post of Ober-Procurator, and his place was taken by Prof. A. V. Kartashev, an outstanding figure in ecclesiastical and civic affairs, and former assistant to the Ober-Procurator. Kartashev was not altogether opposed to the views of his predecessor on the role of the State in the carrying out of ecclesiastical reform. In Kartashev's opinion it was in the interest of the Church itself, as it moved from its position of subservience to the State toward a free organization based on the elective process, that the Provisional Government should remain for a time, as it were "illegally," within the apparatus of ecclesiastical government... and should, "like a midwife," assist in the birth of the conciliar reform of the Church. "Only by this 'surgical expedient' was it possible to hasten the liquidation of the oppressive elements inherited from the old order."[50] He believed that the forthcoming Council, as the constituent assembly of the Russian Church, must submit any legislation it might prepare to the Provisional Government for approval, and only after this could the Church move on to the position of a free, self-governing organization. After that the Government's function would be limited to assuring the legality of the actions of the Church. So long as new laws were being developed for the administration of the Church, however, the Provisional Government must not give up its solicitude for the Church's affairs and interests.

In spite of this the relations of the Holy Synod and the Ober-Procurator took a decided turn for the better under Kartashev. Since he regarded the title of Ober-Procurator as a synonym for the burdensome dependence of the Church on the State, Kartashev renounced it and ten days after his appointment to this office he took the position of Minister of Confessions.

On August 12th, 1917, the Holy Synod passed the "Statute for a Local Council of the Orthodox All Russian Church" introducing only minor changes in the draft set forth by the Pre-Council Consultation. The Holy

Synod admitted, of course, that the "right of composing" such a Statute "belonged to the Council itself," but at the same time it felt that "prior to any Statute it might prepare, the Council would be in need of certain guiding rules," and that this Regulation would serve until there was such an official Statute of the Local Council.

This essentially preliminary and provisional Statute was from the very beginning accepted as a guide by the Council itself and became the chief element in the new and fundamental law of the Russian Church.

The Sacred Council of the Russian Orthodox Church opened in Moscow on August 15th, 1917.

IX

The Statute of the Local Council of the Russian Orthodox Church and the Regulations on Elections

ACCORDING TO THE STATUTE of the Local Council of the Orthodox All Russian Church of August 12th, and also the Regulation on the convocation of such a Council dated July 5th of the same year, the Council was to be organized on quite different principles than those accepted either by the majority or the minority of the members of the Pre-Council Committee of 1906. Under the new regulations the Council of the All Russian Church was not an assembly at which matters would be decided by the bishops alone, with the clergy and laity having only a consultative voice. Nor was it to be a Council where matters could be decided by a majority of the votes of the clergy and laity together with the bishops, putting the latter in the role simply of advisors with no real power to exercise their episcopal authority. The new and modified organization of the Council was the result of an original synthesis of the views of the majority and the minority groups of the Pre-Council Committee of 1906.

In view of the separation of the Church from the State under the non-confessional Provisional Government, and also in light of the process already begun of depriving the Orthodox Church of the privileges it once enjoyed, in consideration of the loss of the generous support of the old government, the Church decided to rely on all its members in the conflict that had already started, drawing them into a living and active participation in the Church's work and bringing all their forces to the defense of its existence. What helped in all this was that not only among the clergy but also among the laity there was a very powerful desire to assist the Church in its efforts to overcome the constantly growing difficulties in which it found itself and to preserve the essential spiritual values of Orthodoxy. The Sacred Council of the Russian Church was seen as a center around which the bishops, clergy and laity could unite in the task of serving the Church, with each of these three groups coming forward as the bearer of its own special privileges and responsibilities in the building up of the Church. All this involved changes: a) in the manner in which the clergy and laity were to be brought into the Council; and b) in the relationship of their powers as members of the Council with the powers of the bishops.

According to the regulations of the Pre-Council Committee of 1906, both clergy and laity, being full members of the Church, were to be included in the Council after a selection by the diocesan bishop from 20-30 candidates presented to him by the deanery conventions. In elections to the Council of 1917, however, the episcopal approval of elected delegates was completely eliminated; once elected, they were recognized as representatives of the clergy and laity of the diocese. At the same time it was decided that there should be an equal number of representatives—three clerics and three laymen—from every diocese.

Since all diocesan bishops were members of the Council ex-officio two clerics and three laymen were to be elected from each diocese. There was a three-stage elective process. A general meeting in each parish elected lay representatives to take part in a deanery electoral convention, attended also by all members of the clergy from parishes in the deanery. The deanery convention then sent its elected representatives to the diocesan electoral convention. Representatives of theological schools of the diocese also took part in this convention. The diocesan electoral convention then chose the delegates to the Council. From the clergy one delegate was chosen from the presbyterate, while the second delegate could be from the ranks of the episcopate (a vicar or retired bishop), or a priest or a deacon. Psalmists could also be elected as representatives of the clergy (Regulation on the convocation of a Local Council, Art. 61-62). At the Council there were delegates also from monks, from the army and navy chaplains, from Edinovertsy (Old-Believers united with the Orthodox Church), and from the Theological Academies. In addition, State institutions of higher learning—the Academy of Science and each university was invited to send one delegate to the Council. Fifteen seats were allotted to Orthodox members of the State Duma and the State Council. Members of the Holy Synod and the Pre-Council Consultation were regarded as members of the Council ex-officio. Beyond this persons especially invited to the Council, representatives of the Eastern Patriarchs and the autocephalous Orthodox Churches were given the right to attend the Council as members. Thus the composition of the Council was such that it could not only express the mind of the whole Russian Church, but also help to further its ties with other Orthodox Local Churches.

Unlike the regulations of the Pre-Council Committee of 1906, the present Council Statute gave the clergy and laity not a consultative but a decisive voice. On the basis of the acts of the Councils of the first nine centuries it is difficult to establish the rights of the clergy and laity with any accuracy. We do not have sufficient evidence to say whether in that period there was a sharp distinction between a decisive and consultative voice. In a mixed Council, of course, no decision could be finally adopted against the will of the bishops and without their consent. On the other hand, the bishops were obliged in some way to coordinate their thinking with that of the clergy and laity. Otherwise what purpose was there in inviting them to such "common consultations" (as St. Cyprian called them)?[51] It is possible that this uncertainty in the relationship of the various groups at the Councils, coupled with the growing authority of the episcopate, were the main causes of the discontinuation of participation in Councils of clergy and laity. The increasing influence of the State on the Church led in later times to a replacement of the laity by representatives of civil authority and the ruling class. If we turn to the Apostolic Council in Jerusalem, we can see that in spite of the lack of equality of its members, in spite of the leading role of the apostles and presbyters in the proposing and making of decisions, the power of the apostles and presbyters was still not above "the general agreement of the whole Church." The decision really came out of this general agreement of the whole assembly, which included precisely "the brethren," and this assent of the people was essential.[52]

The decision of the Pre-Council Committee to give no decisive vote whatever on any occasion to the clergy or the laity was fraught with dangers. The granting of only a consultative voice to these two groups could not fail to result in a divergence of view with the bishops on some questions, a divergence having solid theoretical foundations in the event that among the clergy and laity there should be men with a broad theological background. The simple suppression of their opinions under the overwhelming weight of episcopal opinion could sow the seeds of division and rancor instead of unity, and in the last analysis could lead to a very widespread loss of interest in the whole idea of a Local Council among the people, and also to the weakening of the authority and role of the Council in the Church's life. As the living unity of all the faithful not only in faith and prayer, but also in work, the Church can not be established strictly on the principle of subordination and obedience. What is needed is an immediate awareness of community and unity in the work of all members of the Church. Nor can active participation develop without allowing some individual initiative, without the opportunity of fixing specific goals and working toward them, and without participation in guiding the movement of the work—all of which does not exclude, of course, the need for measures to prevent attempts to take advantage of the rights thus given to the detriment of the good order of the Church.

This granting to the clergy and laity of the right to a decisive vote in the Council was, of course, an essential broadening of their powers as compared with those ascribed to them by the Pre-Council Committee. But even for the latter there was no doubt that the very fact that the clergy and laity were members of the Church meant also that they could be members of a Council. In this regard the Pre-Council Committee upheld the spirit of the Orthodox doctrine that the sacred dignity may belong not only to the clergy who are called to administer the Sacraments, teach, and watch over the souls of their flocks and guide them, but also to the laity, as to "a holy priesthood," "living stones" in the spiritual house (I Pet. 2:5). Thus the laity participate in celebrating divine services with the clergy, they may assist the clergy in spreading and elaborating the Church's doctrine, as well as take part in ecclesiastical administration.

For the Pre-Council Committee what was unacceptable was the broadening of the powers of the clergy and laity to the point of suggesting the equality or identity of their position with that of the bishops, which would really be a "violation of the fundamental principles of ecclesiastical life." The authors of the new Council Statute were confronted therefore with the task of reconciling the granting of a decisive vote to the clergy and laity with the supremacy of the episcopate, and they found a special way of resolving this difficult problem.

Having given the same voting rights to the clergy and the laity as to the bishops, the new Council Statute simultaneously granted the bishops the right to veto any decision of the General Assembly of the Council that seemed to them unacceptable. According to the Council Statute all bishops present at the Council formed a special "Bishop's Conference," which would "consider each decision of the General Assembly of the Council, which establishes general rules or fundamental principles of ecclesiastical organization, and measure its agreement with the Word of God, the canons, the dogmas and the tradition of the Church." (Statute Art. 64). "If in the period of three days from the time of its coming under the consideration of the Bishops Conference, such a decision shall be rejected either in whole or in part by a three-quarters majority of those present in the session of the Conference, with grounds given for such action, then such decision shall be returned to the General Assembly of the Council for review. Any new conciliar decision shall be referred again to the Bishops' Conference" (Statute, p. 65-66). "If after this the decision is again rejected in the Bishops' Conference, then it shall not acquire the force of a conciliar definition, and this fact shall be published at the next meeting of the Council." (Statute, p. 67).

This arrangement guaranteed the supremacy of the episcopate. It not only removed any suppression of the voice of the bishops by that of the clergy and laity, but also made impossible the adoption by the Council of any decision unacceptable to the bishops and not approved by them. However, the bishops could only accept or reject those decisions which had first been adopted by the General Assembly of the Council, where the bishops sat side by side with the clergy and laity. In practice therefore every decision of the Council had to be an expression of the singleness of mind and common accord of the whole Church: bishops, clergy and laity. If this unanimity was not achieved on the first vote, a decision must be placed a second time under the consideration of the General Assembly of the Council so that, in the exchange of views between bishops, clergy and laity, a new decision could be found that was acceptable to both sides. If there was no common accord, no decree could be passed.

The right of the bishops to reject a decision of the General Assembly of the Council was in a sense restricted by the rule that decisions of the Bishops' Conference be adopted by a three quarters majority of votes instead of an absolute majority, as provided in the proposed Statute of the Pre-Council Consultation, which was altered in this and in several other points by the Holy Synod in its meetings on the 10-11th of August, 1917. Furthermore, on the basis of Article 64 of the Statute, the bishops could reject only those decisions, which would establish "general rules or fundamental principles" of Church organization, i.e., general norms of legislative character. This would not include minor decisions of more administrative character concerning particular actions or persons, as for example the election of a certain person for a specific office, or decisions concerning the organization of religious processions, the arranging of an appeal, etc. Also the basis for rejecting a decision could only be its inconsistency with "the Word of God, the dogmas, canons and tradition of the Church." These limitations could have greatly complicated and hindered the work of the Council. They did not have this effect to any great degree, however, as a result of the lofty aspirations of the Council members and their vigorous efforts to renew and strengthen the Church's organization at a critical moment in the life of the Russian Church.

This was a new way of resolving the question of the relations of bishops, clergy and laity at Church Councils, hitherto unknown in the practice of the Orthodox Church.

Up to the twentieth century joint meetings of the episcopate with preponderant numbers of the clergy and laity functioned mainly as meetings for the selection of a Head of the Church: the Patriarch of Constantinople (according to the law of 1860); the Metropolitan of Serbia (law of 1890); of Bulgaria (law of 1895); or of Romania (law of 1872). These councils elected candidates only. A synod of bishops sometimes took part in the complicated process of election, as a governing college, but the actual appointment of a person to the position of Head of a Church depended in the last analysis on civil authority: on the Sultan or the King.

General Church Councils of bishops, clergy and laity were held also in the small Orthodox Churches within the borders (as they existed then) of Austria-Hungary, in the Metropolitanates of Karlovtsy and Sibiu. These councils not only elected the Metropolitan, but also dealt with a vast range of ecclesiastical and administrative matters having to do with the organization of the Orthodox Church in the predominantly Roman Catholic Austro-Hungarian State. Two thirds of the members of these general ecclesiastical councils were laymen and only one third came from the clergy. A small number of bishops filled up the number of these councils, representing a tiny minority. Not only the voice of the bishops but even the voice of all the clergy together could always be silenced by the laity, and in this way the Orthodox principles of the unity of all the members of the Church and the supremacy of the episcopate were distorted. The Council Statute of 1917 found a way of preserving both these principles by giving all the members of the Council a decisive vote and by reserving special restraining powers to the Conference of Bishops.

The General Assembly of the Council and the Bishops' Conference have been seen by some as two chambers in a parliamentary structure.[53] But to speak as if the Council Statute of August 12th, 1917 had established a bicameral system of government is to lose sight of the distinctive features of this Statute and its genuine originality.

Under a bicameral system each of the two chambers has its own special membership, and the members of one chamber must not be members of the other. Each chamber meets separately and makes its decisions apart from the other. In the event of a disagreement on a given law, conference committees are formed to work out a compromise. But the proposals of such a committee are returned for review by each chamber separately, and they are passed or defeated by the votes of the members of each chamber separately.

The Bishops' Conference is not a second chamber, like the House of Bishops of the Episcopal Church in America, which exists alongside the House of Deputies, made up of representatives of the lower clergy and laity. It would be possible to speak of the General Assembly of the Council as a separate chamber only if it was composed solely of clergy and laity, and met apart from the bishops. The Conference of Bishops could be a kind of second chamber only if all the bishops of the Church always met apart from the clergy and laity. But according to Article 1 of the Regulation of July 5th, 1917, "the Council consists of bishops, clergy and laity." The bishops are just as much members of the Council as the clergy and laity. Jointly with them the bishops meet in the General Assembly and on the commissions of the Council. In the consideration of particular questions the bishops have an opportunity to exercise influence on the thinking of the other members of the Council. This influence can be all the more persuasive when the clergy and laity come, as they must, to see the necessity of reconciling their view, in a given question, with that of the bishops. The bishops vote along with the clergy and laity in the General Assembly, and their vote is counted along with all the other votes cast by the members of the Council.

Only after the meeting of the General Assembly of the Council are separate meetings of the Conference of Bishops arranged. The bishops are included in this Conference not because they rule a particular diocese (as was the case in the Council of Bishops), but by reason of the fact that they are members of the Council. Vicar and retired bishops are also members of the Conference. Article 61 of the Statute says that the Conference of Bishops is composed "of all bishops taking part in the Council and having rights to Council membership." The Conference is therefore simply a separate meeting of a special group of members of the Council, a group which realizes its functions, however, within the general framework of the Council's activity as a whole. The Conference of Bishops can make its decisions only as long as the Council is in session, and then within a short three day period. The functions of the Conference of Bishops come to end when the sessions of the Council come to an end. The Council Statute does not envision any kind of conciliation committee to resolve differences.

The decisions of the Sacred Council constitute single acts, each one including the decision of the General Assembly of the Council (made up of bishops, clergy and laity) and the decision of the Bishops' Conference. The

46

Sacred Council of the Russian Church is a single ecclesiastical chamber, in which the episcopal members are given the right to control and guide its legislative activity.

X

The Council's Reorganization of Ecclesiastical Administration

THE REORGANIZATION of the Russian Church was not completed by installing the Sacred Council within the Church's administrative system. The fulfillment of the process of reorganization was left to the Council itself, regarded as a constituent assembly. It "possessed full ecclesiastical authority to organize Russian ecclesiastical life on the basis of the Word of God, the dogmas, canons and tradition of the Church." (Art. 1, Statute).

Since every Local Council is a temporary organization, convened for a specific period of time, it was important at the very outset to create permanent organs for the day to day administration of the Church. These came to be the Sacred Synod and the Supreme Ecclesiastical Council. The way in which they were organized and the procedures established for their work bear witness again to the supremacy of the episcopate which is so characteristic of Orthodoxy, even with the inclusion of lower clergy and laity in these central bodies of the Church.

The Sacred Synod was created as an exclusively hierarchical body.[54] It was composed of the Patriarch, the Metropolitan of Kiev, six bishops chosen by the Sacred Council and five diocesan bishops called to its meetings on a regular rotation basis. This Synod of Twelve bishops, under the presidency of the Patriarch, had the right to deal with matters of doctrine, liturgical order, religious education in the Church-related schools, the approval of diocesan bishops, the appointment of chief officers of institutions placed within the jurisdiction of the Synod, the general supervision of diocesan administration and the monasteries, the missionary work of the Church, and several other administrative and disciplinary matters. The Sacred Synod was the direct descendent of the Councils of Bishops, which from the most ancient times have been the organs of hierarchical guidance in the life of the Local Churches. The rather large membership of the Sacred Synod, the election of some of its personnel by the whole Sacred Council, and the alternating terms of its other members strengthened the ties between the Sacred Synod and the episcopate and also the Church as a whole. But this was not an All

47

Russian Council of ruling diocesan bishops. An All Russian Council of Bishops was anticipated only under such exceptional circumstances as the trial of a Patriarch (Definition of the rights and duties of the Patriarch, Art. 10).

In the ongoing business of ecclesiastical administration and discipline the Sacred Synod would make decisions which by nature would not come within the competence of the Sacred Council, as a legislative body convened periodically and for a limited period of time. Besides these special administrative functions, however, the Sacred Synod was invested also with legislative powers in questions of doctrine, morals, liturgical order, and the preservation of the text of the books of Holy Scripture. In these areas the Sacred Synod could act independently of the Sacred Council, so that alongside the Sacred Council there was created a second legislative body having authority to deal with questions connected with the "spiritual" guidance of the Church.

Not all aspects of ecclesiastical administration were to be supervised immediately by the Sacred Synod. Some matters were placed in the hands of the Supreme Ecclesiastical Council. The Moscow Council was following here a characteristic practice of the time, which admitted a dualism in the permanent administrative bodies of the Church, that is, the formation of a mixed council of bishops, clergy and laity for dealing with "temporal" matters alongside an exclusively hierarchical body, the Synod of Bishops, called to handle the more obviously "spiritual" questions. This approach received a very clear expression in the Canonisms of the Church in Constantinople in 1860, which established both an episcopal Synod and a mixed Council of twelve members. In the same way there was a Conciliar Committee in the Metropolitanate of Karlovtsy (law of 1875), and an Exarchate's Council in the Bulgarian Exarchate (laws of 1871, 1898). In all these mixed councils laymen were in the majority: four bishops and eight laymen in the mixed Council in Constantinople; two bishops, two presbyters and five laymen in the Conciliar Committee of Karlovtsy; one bishop and six laymen in the Council of the Bulgarian Exarchate.[55]

Bishops, clergy and laity were brought together in the Russian Supreme Ecclesiastical Council; specifically, there were three bishops, selected by the Sacred Synod, six members of the clergy, and six laymen, all chosen by the Sacred Council, with the Patriarch as president. The laity had an equal number of representatives with the lower clergy. The clerical element was augmented by the presence of the three bishops and the Patriarch. The Supreme Ecclesiastical Council was called upon to deal with the economic affairs of the Church, the raising of funds for ecclesiastical needs, the management of schools and publications, legal matters involving the Church,

48

the supervision of the accounts of diocesan institutions, etc. An absolute delineation of "temporal" and "spiritual" matters is of course out of the question. A distinction is possible only if one element prevails noticeably over the other. "Temporal" matters serve the interests of the Church, so that the "spiritual" element in them is always clear. It was as an expression of this fact that the Supreme Ecclesiastical Council was formed so that the bishops and other clergy were given an opportunity to exercise a real influence on the decisions made in this Council.

This was not all that was accomplished, however, by the Council of 1917-1918. Joint meetings of the Sacred Synod and the Supreme Ecclesiastical Council were also provided for the consideration of major economic and administrative questions, of concern to the whole Church. The approval of the budgets of ecclesiastical institutions, the examination of the accounts of the Sacred Synod and the Supreme Ecclesiastical Council, the appointment of persons in charge of the central institutions of the Church, and a number of other questions were placed in the hands of the Joint Committee of the Sacred Synod and the Supreme Ecclesiastical Council. Its membership consisted of the Patriarch, twelve bishops, six lower clergy and six laymen, giving the bishops ample opportunity to influence the Committee's decisions.

The creation of these various organs in the supreme administration of the Church naturally brought about the need for a special institution which could unify their activities and insure that all were working in the same general direction. "What is needed is a permanent center of conciliar unity, someone who will draw together the scattered flock" (Prince E. N. Trubetskoy). When the subjugation of the Church's administration to the State was brought to an end and the Church's self-government restored, there was a need for an authoritative representative and spokesman of the Church — especially in its dealing with the State. We must also take into consideration the special circumstances existing when the definitions of the supreme administrative bodies of the Church were adopted. The Bolshevist Revolution had begun to spread across the land, and heavy clouds were building up over the Church. More than ever before the need was felt for a leader around whom the people of the Church could unite. "We need a Patriarch, as one who will stand for the Russian Church in ecclesiastical and liturgical matters, a man of stature and daring, a defender of the Russian Church." "When there is a war, a single leader is necessary; without such a man, the army falls into disorder." This was the sentiment of the Council.[56]

In the course of its deliberations the Moscow Council had arrived here at the point of recognizing an extraordinary elevated spiritual authority in the Church, that is, the very powerful figure of a Patriarch, who would not only be the Primate and Spiritual Head of the Church, but also a Ruler vested with broad powers over both central and local organs of the Church, as well as the right of supervision of the personal life and administrative conduct of the Church's bishops. ("Definition of the rights and duties of the Most Holy Patriarch," Dec. 8, 1917, Art. 1-4).

The elevation of the Patriarch above all the central administrative bodies of the Church was further assured by the very means used for his se-lection. Three candidates for the Patriarchate were elected by the whole Sacred Council: bishops, clergy and laity. Then, following the example of the selection of the Apostle Matthias (Acts 1:23-26), lots were drawn to determine which of the three was to be Patriarch. On the first choice the lot fell on the name of Metropolitan Tikhon (Belavin) of Moscow. "The Most Holy Patriarch of Moscow and all Russia" was called to unify the activities of all supreme administrative bodies of the Church as President of the Local Council, the Sacred Synod, the Supreme Ecclesiastical Council, and also the Joint Committee of the Synod and Council. Only the Patriarch could call a Local Council, although he could influence its decisions only as one of the members of the Conference of Bishops. In the Sacred Synod, the Supreme Ecclesiastical Council and their Joint Committee, however, he was given the special right to protest decisions whenever he found that they "did not serve the interests and welfare of the Church." This right of protest could, therefore, be used by the Patriarch not only when decisions were contrary to law, but also when they were, in his opinion, not advisable for practical reasons.

In the last analysis a protest by the Patriarch could nullify a decision made in these bodies. The protested decision would be sent back for recon-sideration by the body from which it had come. "If, however, the Patriarch shall find it impossible to agree with the revised decision, then either a) the final resolution of the question shall be postponed; or b) the matter shall be transferred to and finally disposed of by the next All Russian Local Council; or c) the Patriarch shall make his own independent decision on the matter, and this decision shall be carried out." Any such decision made by the Patriarch could be brought up for review in the next All Russian Council. (Art. 20 of the "Definition of the Sacred Synod and the Supreme Ecclesiastical Council," Dec. 7, 1917). This meant that in the event of a postponement of a decision without its transfer to the next Council for final disposition, the decision could not come into effect; even if transferred to a subsequent Council for review, it would have no force until the actual con-vocation of the Council. In any case, the supreme bodies of the Church were in no position to execute any order or decree without the approval of the Patriarch. If the Patriarch should make an "independent decision," it could have force up to the time of the next Council not only without the agreement of the Sacred Synod and the Supreme Ecclesiastical Council, but even against their will.

This extraordinary extension of the powers of the Patriarch may be justified by the abnormal conditions of the war against religion that was about to be undertaken by the atheistic communist power. If the organs of ecclesiastical administration were destroyed or scattered the Patriarch would be in a position to act apart from them and in their stead. Under more normal and peaceful conditions the Patriarch would have substantial power to influence these supreme administrative bodies only through the right of protest.

Under the conditions fixed by the Council the right of protest was tantamount to the confirmation by the Patriarch of the decisions of the Sacred Synod and the Supreme Ecclesiastical Council. It should be noted, however, that this right had reference to decisions of the Sacred Synod, as the permanent executive committee of bishops administering the Church's affairs, but not to the General Council of all ruling bishops in the Church. Such a Council is mentioned only as the body in which a Patriarch could be brought to trial.

The regulations governing such a General Council of Bishops were not sufficiently elaborated, and as a periodically convened assembly of the whole episcopate it was not included in the general scheme of the Church's supreme administration. A relatively small Synod of Bishops can actually constitute a General Council of Bishops in small Churches having only a few ruling diocesan bishops — as in the Church of Cyprus (with four bishops). For the Russian Church, however, which had at that time sixty-five dioceses and three foreign missions headed by bishops, the Sacred Synod of twelve bishops could not take the place of a General Council of all ruling bishops. The canons and practice of the Orthodox Church do not anticipate Patriarchal approval of decisions adopted by a General Council of Bishops as the supreme hierarchal authority of a Local Church invested with every important administrative functions. Such approval would violate the principle of the supremacy of the episcopate as a whole. If a General Council of all ruling bishops were included in the overall system of ecclesiastical administration, the Patriarch could have the right in case of necessity to transfer the decisions of the permanent Synod of Bishops to the General Council of Bishops. In such a case the Synod would not, of course, consist of twelve bishops (as in Russia), but of a much smaller number.

There was then a very characteristic change in the definition of the limits of the Patriarch's authority. The Pre-Council Committee of 1906 regarded the Patriarch as a First Hierarch, as President of the Council and the Synod, as the supreme overseer of the good order of the Church, as one who could urge the Synod to pass measures for the restoration of good order. It did not, however, give him any power whatever over the decisions of the permanent Synod, or still less over those of the Council of Bishops. On November 4th, 1917, the Moscow Council accepted the Patriarch as "first among the bishops, who are equal to him," accountable to the Local Council, as were the other supreme administrative bodies of the Church (Art. 3-4). Yet little more than a month later, on Dec. 7th of the same year, it gave him a right of protest which raised him above the Sacred Synod of twelve bishops and also above the Supreme Ecclesiastical Council. This was done not only because the convocation of another Council, to which he would be accountable, seemed in those turbulent times to be postponed indefinitely, but also because of the peculiarities of the newly created ecclesiastical organization, which made a single organ for unifying the supreme administration of the Church a genuine necessity.

The Primate of Orthodox Local Churches is chosen, according to a common rule, for life. Like any other bishop, however, he can be tried by a Council of Bishops for failure to carry out his duties or for preaching heretical doctrines. The Moscow Council of 1917-1918 set the Patriarch's authority above that of the Sacred Synod, partly by granting him the right to protect and also by the very means of his election by the whole Sacred Council. It also sought to protect the Patriarch's authority by refusing to grant to the Sacred Synod itself the right to bring the Patriarch to trial. In the event of his violation of the privileges or responsibilities of his office, "three senior members of the Sacred Synod or members of the Supreme Ecclesiastical Council in episcopal orders" could address "brotherly advice" to the Patriarch. If a second "brotherly advice" from the three senior bishops proved unsuccessful, a complaint against the Patriarch could be presented in the Sacred Synod to the senior bishop present. But "the question whether there is any cause for the persecution of the Patriarch," was to be determined not by the Sacred Synod alone, but by the Joint Committee of the Synod and Supreme Ecclesiastical Council, in other words, by the twelve bishops and the twelve members of the Supreme Ecclesiastical Council elected from the clergy and laity. The arraignment and the trial itself were entrusted to the All Russian Council of Bishops, to which, following historical precedent in the Russian Church, other Patriarchs and representatives of autocephalous Churches could be invited. "Moreover both arraignment and the sentencing of a Patriarch must be done by vote of not less than two thirds of the members present." ("Regulations concerning the rights and duties of the Patriarch," Art. 8-10.)

The decrees concerning the Patriarch, the Sacred Synod and the Supreme Ecclesiastical Council were significant not just because they created certain permanent organs of ecclesiastical administration alongside the Sacred Council, called periodically and for a limited term. These decrees also gave more precise definition of the powers of the Council and introduced some restrictions in its function.

It was at the Pre-Council Conference of 1906 that it was first suggested that, as the highest organ of the Church, a Council should have not only legislative authority, but also governmental, judicial and supervisory powers.[58] At that time such a unification of all powers seemed perfectly natural, inasmuch as the decisions of the Council were to be made by bishops only, with bishops having also the right to judge bishops. In 1917 this idea was applied to a Council having a completely different membership. The Definition of the Supreme Administration of the Orthodox Russian Church of Nov. 4, 1917, read: "In the Orthodox Russian Church the supreme authority — legislative, administrative, judicial and supervisory — belongs to the Local Council, as convened periodically, and including in its membership bishops, clergy and laity."

If we place this order side by side with two other definitions published in the same month, the first concerning the sphere of activity coming within the competence of the Sacred Synod (Dec. 8th, 1917) and the second dealing with the trial of a Patriarch, it is easy to see that legislative power can belong to the Council only in those matters which do not come directly within the competence of the Synod. In the prescribed fields of doctrine and ecclesiastical administration committed to the Sacred Synod, the Synod is free to act in complete independence, although nothing prohibits it from referring certain questions — for one reason or another — to the whole Sacred Council. The administrative authority remains with the Sacred Council not in the sense of carrying on the regular tasks of administration committed to the Patriarch, the Sacred Synod and the Supreme Ecclesiastical Council, but in the sense that the Council preserves the right to resolve, by legislation, general questions of an organizational nature; and can modify or supplement existing regulations concerning such things as the central and local organs of the Church, the Church's entry into various types of union with other Churches or ecclesiastical organizations, the preservation of the Church's wholeness and independence, and its relationships with institutions of the State. The judicial functions of the Sacred Council were naturally limited by the regulations on the trial of a Patriarch by the All Russian Council of Bishops, and would be limited still more by the creation of the Supreme Ecclesiastical Court.

The Moscow Council did not succeed in working out a general Regulation dealing with ecclesiastical courts; it only transferred the function of the Diocesan Court to an elected administrative body under the Bishop of the Diocese, called the Diocesan Council (Art. 58). The supervisory power of the Council, finally, could be exercised now only in its evaluation of the reports of organs accountable to the Council. (Regulations concerning the Sacred Synod and Supreme Ecclesiastical Council, Dec. 7th, 1917, Art 2). After its consideration of these reports, the Sacred Council passes its own resolutions regarding them.

As a result, the Sacred Council became a legislative body mainly in the realm of the organization of ecclesiastical administration. Questions of doctrine and spiritual guidance were transferred to the Sacred Synod of Bishops. Because of its general structure, the Council could not exercise its judicial powers. We may suppose that in the final draft of legislation on ecclesiastical courts the functions of a supreme court would also have been transferred to other institutions, just as the trial of a Patriarch had been transferred to the All Russian Council of Bishops.

XI

The Results of the Moscow Council of 1917-1918

A LONG PERIOD OF PREPARATION was needed to bring into being the Sacred Council of the Russian Church. In the nineteenth century the Russian Church reached its highest point of development, not only in the size of its membership, which exceeded the total membership of all other Local Orthodox Churches combined, but also in the high level of learning of its bishops and clergy, in the development of theological studies, and in the aroused interest in the Church among the common people and the Russian intelligentsia. The Russian Church of that time was able to make its own contributions to the question of the canonical organization of the Orthodox Church within the conditions of contemporary life. Herein lay the significance of the "Statute of the Local Council," with its Regulations on membership, and also of the decrees adopted by the Council on the subject of the Patriarch and the supreme administrative bodies of the Church.

The Church lives its own special life, apart from the life of the State, and has its own way of measuring the events of this world. In spite of all the attempts on the part of the State to lay its hands on the reorganization of the Church's administrative structure, the Holy Synod has kept the work of reform in its own hands. The common spirit that moved the bishops, clergy and laity of the Church is reflected in their understanding and defense of the Church's interests in the Pre-Council Consultation of 1917 and in the Council itself. For all their keen awareness of the contemporary situation, the leaders of the Church in that time did not forsake the traditional foundation of Orthodox Church structure—the supremacy of the episcopate —and they created a new and more complete system for bringing together the episcopate, the clergy and the laity in the central administrative bodies of the Church. The Moscow Council proceeded, again in its own way, to the election of a Patriarch. It chose as candidates for this office men who were least acceptable to the Provisional Government — among them Archbishop Antony (Khrapovitsky) and Metropolitan Tikhon (Belavin) of Moscow. The latter had been dismissed from the Sacred Synod by the Ober-Procurator V. N. Lvov, and yet he subsequently occupied the See of the Patriarch of Moscow and All Russia. Drawing conclusions from the shifting turn of events which marked this period, we may note the following basic features of the newly created administrative structure which took the place of the synodal system:

1) The uniting of bishops, clergy and laity in the Sacred Council, each being given a decisive vote in the General Assembly of the Council, and the granting to the Conference of Bishops of the right to reject the decisions of the General Assembly of the Council.

2) The acceptance of the principle of equality of representation from the clergy and laity with the admission of supplementary representation from other ecclesiastical organizations.

3) The retention of broad powers by the Sacred Synod of Bishops, in the field of doctrine and worship, as well as in matters of ecclesiastical administration and discipline; so that the Sacred Synod evolved as a special legislative organ in spiritual matters alongside the Sacred Council, the latter being left to deal with broad organizational questions.

4) The creation of the Supreme Ecclesiastical Council, with a mixed membership, to handle matters of a basically "economic" nature, as distinct from the Sacred Synod, which was designed to deal with those other matters of ecclesiastical administration which had been assigned to it.

5) The formation of the Joint Committee of the Sacred Synod and the Supreme Ecclesiastical Council for the examination of the more important questions of the Church's business.

6) The setting up of a special procedure for the election of a Patriarch by the whole Council (including bishops, clergy and laity) ; the granting to the Patriarch — as the person unifying all the activities of the supreme bodies within the Church's administration — of the right to preside over these bodies; and the bestowal upon him of the right to protest or suspend the decisions of the permanent administrative institutions of the Church.

While including the clergy and laity in the various central organs of the Church's administration, and retaining also the supremacy of the episcopate, with its exclusive powers in the realms of doctrine and spiritual oversight, the Moscow Council succeeded also in substantially elevating the power of the Patriarch.

The reorganization of the structure of the Russian Church by the Statute of 1917 and the decrees of the Moscow Council of 1917-1918 were a part of a clearly revealed movement toward the inclusion of the clergy and laity in the supreme administrative bodies of Orthodox Local Churches. After the abolition of the Canonisms of 1860 the Patriarchate of Constantinople returned to the former system of governing through a Synod (or Council) of Bishops. This same system, with supreme administrative bodies exclusively episcopal in character, was preserved also in the Churches of Greece and Cyprus. In the meantime, the Romanian (1925), Serbian (1931 and 1947) and Syrian-Antiochian (1929 and 1955) Patriarchates began to include clergy and laity not only in assemblies for the election of the Head of the Church, but also in some of the highest ecclesiastical bodies, establishing various forms and conditions under which they could participate. Later on the decrees of the Moscow Council of 1917-1918 have been reflected in the Statutes of Churches behind the Iron Curtain: in Russia (1945), Romania (1949), Bulgaria (1951), and also in the Churches of Poland and Czechoslovakia, although the oppressive measures of the communist regime have in many respects distorted the position of the episcopate, as well as that of the clergy and laity. Within these Churches a certain increase in the role of the episcopate can still be discerned, however, since the communist authorities find it more convenient to deal with a centralized ecclesiastical authority concentrated in the hands of the bishops.

As a result of the cruel persecutions of the Church under the Soviet Government, the ecclesiastical structure established in 1917-1918 could not

56

be consolidated within Russia itself. Its fundamental principles have been received, however, by two parts of the Russian Church abroad: The Western European Metropolitan District, and the American Metropolitanate.

NOTES

1 A. V. Kartashev, *Ocherki po istorii Russkoy Tserkvi,* ("Essay on the History of Russian Church") Vol. II, Paris, 1959, pp. 349-350, 389-391, 424-425.

2 G. Florovsky, *Puti russkogo bogoslovia,* ("Pathways of Russian Theology"), Paris, 1937, pp. 152, 200 ff.

3 N. S. Sushkov, *Zapiski o zhizni i vremeni Moskovskogo Mitropolita Filareta,* ("Notes on the Life and Times of Metropolitan Filaret of Moscow"), Moscow, 1868, pp. 194-196; see also the forward of O. Bodyansky to the article "O sobornom upravlenii," ("Conciliar Government"), in *Chtenia v Imperatorskom Obshchestve istorii i drevnostey Rossiskikh,* ("Journal of the Imperial Society for the Study of Russian History and Archeology"), 1870, Bk. IV, pp. iii-iv.

4 A. Papkov, *Tserkovno-obshchestvennye voprosi v epokhu Tsarya Osvoboditelya,* ("Ecclesiastical and Social Problems at the Times of the Tsar-Liberator"), St. Petersburg, 1902, pp. 20-21.

5 *Ibid.,* 19-31; *Sobranie mneniy i otzyvov Mitropolita Filareta,* ("Opinions and papers of Metropolitan Filaret"), Bk. IV, pp. 213, 225, 227; Letters of Metropolitan Arseny, in *Russy Archiv,* ("Russian Archives"), 1892, Bk. II, p. 200 ff; "Pisma Preosvyashchennogo Innokentiya," (Letters of Bishop Innokenty"), to Muravyev, in *Russky Archiv,* ("Russian Archives"), 1889, Nos. 5 and 6.

6 "Plenenie Russkoy Tserkvi," ("The Captivity of the Russian Church"), a memorandum by Archbishop Agafangel of Volhynia. This memorandum remained in manuscript for a long time and was not published until 1906, in Moscow, by S. Sharapov.

7 This work was preserved among the manuscripts left by Metropolitan Isidor to the Library of the St. Petersburg Theological Academy. See Papkov, *Tserkovno-obshchestvennye voprosi,* p. 30.

8 Metropolitan Antony's memorandum was printed in the newspaper *Slovo* on March 28th, 1905. See I. V. Preobrazhensky, *Tserkovnya reforma, sbornik statey dukhovnoy i svetskoy periodicheskoy pechati po voprosu o reforme,* ("Church Reform, A collection of articles in the ecclesiastical and secular press"), St. Petersburg, 1906, pp. 85-89, 133-136.

9 S. Yu. Witte's memorandum was first printed in the newspaper *Slovo* (The Word), also on March 28th, 1905. See Preobrazhensky, *Tserkovnaya reforma,* pp. 122-133.

10 *Tserkovnaya reforma,* pp. 91-93.

11 *Zhurnaly i protokoly zasedanii Predsobornogo Prisutstvia,* ("Minutes of the Sessions of the Pre-Council Committee"), Vol. I. St. Petersburg, 1906, pp. vi-vii.

12 *K Tserkovnomu Soboru; sbornik gruppy Peterburgskikh svyashchennikov,* ("A Church Council; Collection of Articles, published by the Group of Priest of Petersburg"), St. Petersburg, 1906, pp. iii-v, 1-8.

13 Published on March 17th, 1905, in *Tserkovny Vestnik,* (The Church Messenger"), No. 11; see also *Tserkovnaya reforma,* pp. 1-6.

14 *Tserkovnaya reforma,* pp. 85-89, 228-229.

15 *Ibid.*, pp. 199-204, 281-282.

16 *Tserkovny Vestnik*, 1905, No. 21; *K Tserkovnomu Soboru,* pp. 9-23.

17 Bishop Nikon (Rklitsky). *Zhizneopisanie blazhenneishego Antonia, Mitropolita Kievskogo i Galitskogo,* ("Biography of Antony, Metropolitan of Kiev and Galicia"), Vol. III, New York, 1957, pp. 45-55.

18 *K Tserkovnomu soboru,* pp. 62-148.

19 *Zhurnaly i protokoly,* Vol. III, St. Petersburg, 1907, p. 412.

20 *Op. cit.,* Vol. I, St. Petersburg, 1906, pp. 98, 99, 137.

21 *Op. cit.,* Vol. II, p. 581.

22 *Op. cit.,* Vol. I, pp. 9, 10.

23 *Ibid.,* pp. 14, 122, 123.

24 *Ibid.,* p. 146.

25 Prof. A. I. Almazov, *Zhyrnaly i protokoly,* Vol. II, p. 427.

26 *Zhurnaly i protokoly,* Vol. II, pp. 466, 467.

27 *Otzyvy eparkhialnykh arkhiereev o tserkovnoy reforme,* ("Responses of the Diocesan Bishops to the Questions of the Church Reform"), St. Petersburg, Part I, No. 56, p. 195. (cited in *Zhurnaly i protokoly,* Vol. III, p. 86).

28 *Zhurnaly i protokoly,* Vol. II, p. 461.

29 *Ibid.,* pp. 432, 433.

30 *Ibid.,* p. 417.

31 *Ibid.,* p. 433.

32 *Op. cit.,* Vol. I, p. 10.

33 *Op. cit.,* Vol II, p. 423.

34 *Op. cit.,* Vol. I, pp. 581, 582.

35 *Ibid.,* p. 17.

36 *Ibid.,* p. 588.

37 *Ibid.,* Vol. I, pp. 582, 583.

38 *Ibid.,* pp. 582-585.

39 *Ibid.,* pp. 17, 31, 588.

40 *Op. cit.,* Vol. III, pp. 123, 124.

41 *Op. cit.,* Vol. II, pp. 462, 463.

42 *Op. cit.,* Vol. I, pp. 15-32, 116-124; Vol. II, pp. 420-441.

43 *Iid.,* Vol. I, p. 18.

44 *Ibid.,* p. 190.

45 *Op. cit.,* Vol. II, p. 461.

46 *Ibid.* p. 670.

47 *Op. cit.,* Vol. III, p. 384.

48 *Deyaniya Svyashchennogo Sobora Rossiiskoy Tserkvi,* (Acts of the Sacred Council of the Russian Church), Bk. II, Part 2, pp. 154, 155; 163-166; 189-193.

49 A. V. Kartashev, "Revolyutsia i Sobor 1917-1918," ("The Revolution and the Sobor of 1917-1918"), *Bogoslovskaya Mysl,* ("Theological Thoughts"), Paris, 1942, pp. 75-92; John S. Curtis, *The Russian Church and the Soviet State,* Boston, 1953, pp. 9-25; George M. Benigsen, "The Year 1917 in the History of the Russian Church," *St. Vladimir's Seminary Quarterly,* 1963, No. 3, pp. 115-125.

50 A. V. Kartashev, "Vremennoe Pravitelstvo i Tserkov," (The Provisional Government and the Church), in *Sovremennye zapiski,* Vol. 52, pp. 373-377.

51 *Ante-Nicene Fathers,* New York, 1926, Vol. V, p. 294.

52 Veselin Kesich, "The Apostolic Council at Jerusalem," in *St. Vladimir's Seminary Quarterly*, 1962, No. 3, p. 113.

53 A. V. Kartashev, "Revolyutsia i Sobor 1917-1918," *Provoslavnaya Mysl*, ("Orthodox Thought"), 1930, Vol. II, p. 88.

54 The decrees of the 1917-1918 Council dealing with the supreme administration of the Church were printed abroad by the Polish Church, in Warsaw, and also by the Holy Trinity Monastery in Jordanville in 1948, under the title *Tserkovnye Zakony kasayushchiesya Russkoy Pravoslavnoy Tserkvi zagranitsey*.

55 Bishop Nikodim, *Pravoslavnoe tserkovnoe pravo*, ("The Orthodox Ecclesiastical Law"), St. Petersburg, 1897, pp. 341-355; R. Janin, *Les églises orientales*, Paris, 1955, pp. 210-215.

56 *Deyania Svyashchennogo Sobora*, Bk. II, Part 2, p. 235; Bk III, p. 6.

57 *Ibid*. Bk. III, pp. 105-114; A. Wuyts, S. J., "Le patriarcat Russe en Concile de Moscou de 1917-1918," *Orientalia Christiana Analecta*, Roma, 1941, pp. 33-47.

58 *Zhurnaly i protokoly*, Vol. I, pp. 128-130; Vol. II, pp. 609, 616, 672.